"The essence of a joyful business is working with the right clients who bring you joy. Matt's book shows you how to do exactly that."
— Mike Michalowicz, Author of *Get Different and Profit First*

"There are a lot of business books on the tactics of business success. Matt's book gives you that and more. He speaks from the heart about how to have JOY in growing your business. Matt's a guy who brings joy to those around him and will help bring joy and a smile to you as you run your business."
— Ramon Ray, Founder, SmartHustle.com

"Business is people connecting with people and more importantly creating meaningful relationships to create more success for everyone. This book is your roadmap for doing just that. You might call it your roadmap to success, but only if you don't just read the book but apply it."
— Mark Hunter, "The Sales Hunter," Author of *A Mind for Sales*

"Matt Ward breaks it down—a path to a profitable business, but also one that is rewarding and productive. If you're contemplating a business or relatively new to it, you should read this book. If you're really serious, reach out to Matt."
— Frank Agin, President, AmSpirit Business Connections

"I started my business in 2008 and have been through every stage that Matt talks about in *The High-Five Effect* and his descriptions about each one is spot on. As business owners, we often feel isolated and in a bubble because we spend the majority of our time behind a laptop. While we might feel like we are the only ones with these feelings and issues, we are not. Matt's book and philosophy about building solid business relationships is refreshing and encouraging because as humans we need to feel connected to the people we surround ourselves with. We spend more time with our work families than we do with our real families so you better believe that having good relationships with our clients is important to making us happy."
— Ronii Bartles, Business Strategist and Marketing Expert

"I've read so many business books over the years, but this one is different. Matt tells the incredible story of Hershey and how that experience changed his life. Armed with this incredible experience, he started venturing out into the business world. This is a collection of valuable best practices that when applied will help your business grow. You'll fall in love with it as I did. It's going to stay on my desk as a reference for years to come. This is truly business gold!"
— Mike Toy, Author of *The Magic of Influence*

"Matt has done it again in *The High-Five Effect*! Matt has such a way of taking successful business building concepts and breaking them down into easy-to-take action steps. No matter what stage you are at in your small business, *The High-Five Effect* can break down your successes or struggles and help you grow to the next stage! I love how Matt puts focus on the joy and happiness of running a business and why you started your business in the first place! *The High-Five Effect* is a must read for any entrepreneur or small business owner who is looking for more success, more time, more money, more freedom, and ultimately, more joy and happiness from their business! Thank you, Matt!"
— Doug Casault, Consultant, Doug17 Consulting

"Are you anxious and stressed about your business all of the time? All business owners need more joy. It's so easy to work all of the time and get burnt out. This book changes the game! Matt shows you, in an amazing step-by-step guide, how to identify where you are in your business and how to bring joy to your life and business practices."
— Gina Ahtof, Owner of Promo Print Plus

"Matt Ward has hit a home run in his book *The High-Five Effect*. If you are a business owner and have lost your passion for your business, read this book to get inspired. Matt shares that the answer is to find relationships that bring you joy."
— Gary Wilbers, Positive Culture Mentor

"Matt's book delivers practical steps for the small business owner who wants to succeed in today's marketplace. If you want to discover how to build a business that serves people you like and is designed in a way that

gives you what you want (a solid income, flexibility, and less stress), this book is for you."
— Sonja Stetzler, Founder and CEO, Effective Connecting

"Consider this book required reading for all business owners. I see it again and again in my public speaking coaching clients—they've started a business and end up resenting the business. It's not the grind, the hard work, or the herculean confidence it takes to get a business started—it's that they have never stopped to ask which types of customers and team members really bring them JOY! Matt Ward makes the case for chasing joy in our business and then shows you exactly how to do it."
— Mike Ganino, Storytelling Coach and Creator of the Certified Original Method for Public Speakers and Transformational Storytellers

"*The High-Five Effect* provides real, actionable advice to business owners at all stages. Matt masterfully helps the reader to identify where they're at, where they want to be, and steps to take to bridge the gap. As an entrepreneur, my goal is to feel the joy from my business and extend that to my employees and clients. I can't wait to use some of the tactics this book provides in my continued pursuit of happiness (and a vacation)."
— Beth Blaney, CEO of Beth Blaney & Associates

"*The High-Five Effect* was like a breath of fresh air for me. It put me back in control of my business, realizing I didn't have to take on every client who came my way. I could choose the ones who brought me joy, or at least wouldn't drive me crazy. Every page of this book is filled with practical advice that will not only make your business more profitable but give you greater peace of mind, and often that's worth more than the profits."
— Tyler R. Tichelaar, PhD and Award-Winning Author of *The Nomad Editor: Living the Lifestyle You Want, Doing Work You Love*

"*The High-Five Effect* is a must read. This book should be on every leader's desk! Matt Ward shows you what to focus on, stay away from, and what to ultimately drive toward. Improve your organization's culture by focusing on joy and joyful people and watch the improvements in your people, process, and profits."
— Jennifer Elder CSP CPA, Chief Solutions Officer

"I became a fan of Matt's writing with his first book *MORE...: Word of Mouth Referrals, Lifelong Customers & Raving Fans.* His latest endeavor, *The High-Five Effect: How to Do Business with People Who Bring You Joy,* is a much needed, easy-to-follow guide for novice and experienced entrepreneurs on the proper steps to starting and running a business. But perhaps one of the greatest lessons everyone can learn from Matt's writing is how to attract the customers you want most—the customers who will return more, refer more, and bring you the greatest amount of joy to serve."
— Ron Ruth, Creative Customer Experience Design

*"The High-Five Effect* gets right to the heart of what every entrepreneur wants—clients who are a joy to work with. Matt's sage advice helps business owners see how to get out of survival mode and create thriving businesses. Move over *E-Myth Revisited.* Every entrepreneur should read this book."
— Mari Ryan, MBA, MHP, CEO/Founder, AdvancingWellness

"Yes, it's true! There can be JOY in running your business. Relationships are at the core of every service-based business. *The High-Five Effect* offers you insights and practical actions not only to make money in your work (of course) but to nurture your business relationships with consistency and authenticity so you can truly thrive in your business with more time, satisfaction, and most importantly, more freedom."
— Susan Finn, Digital Marketing Strategist, Rise Above Noise

# THE HIGH-FIVE EFFECT

HOW TO DO BUSINESS WITH PEOPLE
WHO BRING YOU JOY

**MATT WARD**

# DEDICATION

I dedicate this book to each and every business owner I've crossed paths with along the way. You have all taught me something.

Some of you taught me exactly what it means to have meaningful relationships where we can high-five...

Some of you taught me about business...

Some of you even broke bread or had a few drinks with me...

And some of you—yeah, I never called you back because you just wanted to pitch me some service you had, and what that really taught me was what *not* to do.

# ACKNOWLEDGMENTS

I would like to thank the following people:

**Lisa March**—My partner in crime who handles so much for me when I'm focused on my business in addition to my clients' businesses. Without you, much of what I do would not be possible.

**David Glickman**—Your work is amazing and has transformed what I do. The seed of this book was planted by you. Your vision for this was spectacular, and I'm grateful for that.

**Tamsen Webster**—Your guidance through the process of developing my ideas has been immeasurable, and I am thankful to call you a friend, colleague, and truth be told, the original "Idea Whisperer™."

Many other people deserve to be acknowledged for their help along the way. My development editor, **Cindy Tschosik**, helped lay out the foundation of the book. A house is always built with a solid foundation; you poured the concrete with me for hours upon hours, flushing out so much. I appreciate you very much.

Special thanks go out to the book editing team at **Superior Book Productions, Tyler Tichelaar and Larry Alexander**, for pulling out all my extra exclamations points!!!! (see what I did there?)

Thank you to **JuLee Brand of designchik** for the great cover and layout design as well as publishing advice and strategy, and **Nicole Connolly** for the great headshot and always making me look better on photos that I do in person!

Additionally, there are dozens and dozens of small business owners who took time out of their busy schedules to be interviewed; to you, I'm thankful.

**And two more people need to be acknowledged—**

**First, that one person I always fail to name.** For you, I'm sorry. I am grateful. I promise. It's just there's a whole lot of words in this book and my mind is racing with excitement. I'm sorry, and I mean it. I'll make it up to you. Just call me!

**Finally...you, the readers. Thank you!**

Without you, the reader and business owner, there would be no book. The fact that people were excited to read this book when the seed was planted means that someone saw value in the idea, and the harvest is this book, which you now have the pleasure of reading.

From the bottom of my heart, and deep in my soul, thank you for reading this. I hope it helps you in some way with your business.

# TABLE OF CONTENTS

# FOREWORD

**Foreword by:** Jason Cutter / Cutter Consulting Group
Sales Consultant, Coach, Trainer, Speaker, and Shark-Tagging Marine
Biologist, Author of *Selling With Authentic Persuasion: Transform from
Order Taker to Quota Breaker*

One side benefit of the global pandemic was it became even easier to
find networking groups around the country, and world, to meet like-
minded individuals. Whether it was for business growth or personal
growth purposes, like most people, I was able to fill my schedule with
so many different meetings. I was not looking to network with the target of finding people who wanted to hire me as an advisor, coach, or
trainer for their sales team. Instead, my focus was to find other great,
motivated, inspiring people doing big things in their lives and businesses. People I would enjoy hanging out with and, if it made sense,
potentially doing business with.

When the pandemic started, I was just over a year into my second attempt at being self-employed. The first time didn't end with
some sexy, big payout exit. It came after two years of struggling to
succeed, with a business partner who was still working his day job
while I was doing my best to figure out how to win the small business
game. Working from home meant I always felt I needed to be working.
What I thought should have been a good income with the freedom
to work when and where I wanted was instead a tough grind without
that great payoff.

Being an only child, my default mode is to go it alone. Mix that
with being raised to have a strong work ethic and I will grind it out to
try to succeed. Of course, that mode doesn't work long-term, and it's
not sustainable.

That first business venture ended silently as I went to work for a
startup, with a base salary, doing similar work to what I was doing in
my business.

My current business is different. Partially because I have sixteen years of experience in companies and in life since then. Partially because I am way more self-aware now and understand my strengths and what value I truly can provide to companies and salespeople.

But mostly because I have realized that two cliché sayings are true: "It's not what you know, it's who you know," and "Your net worth is your network." The mistake I have made before is applying those two axioms with only monetary goals in mind, usually coming from a place of scarcity. This practice has led to starting business and referral relationships with people I don't actually like being around. It has led to taking on clients for the sake of the business value, even though I didn't like their product, culture, and sometimes their team.

Over the last two years, I have realized two things: 1) I know I can provide massive value to my client's business, and when I do my job correctly, I should get compensated well; and 2) Life is too short to do things you hate. And life will feel really long and painful if you have to do business with people you don't like.

Even before I knew about this book, I met Matt in online networking events (I called them "Pandemic Relief" networking groups... which for a lot of people was the only way to get some positive human interaction). In that first event where we were both present (thanks, Frank Agin!), I could instantly tell Matt was going to be fun, and that he was also wanted to build relationships with a long-term goal of referrals.

One of Matt's philosophies that I have appreciated most is his desire to only work with people he enjoys speaking with. It's not just about business with him; it's about working with people who bring you joy. When you have that focus in your relationships, generating money together becomes fun.

*The High-Five Effect* is designed to empower you, the small business owner, with the goal of growing a business (that doesn't feel like an endless grind) that comes from a place of abundance to build relationships that bring you joy first, and then nurture them over the long term. This book was created to give you a framework for trusting that when you stand up for your happiness in relationships, great things will come to you.

# THE SWEET SMELL OF SUCCE$$

*"No matter where you start, you can find Joy in your business."*

— *Matt Ward*

Let me share two examples of very different people, one well-known, one not well known yet! These two individuals were able to find joy and bring joy to others, even though that's likely not what they initially set out to do. They were more than a century apart in age, and one died before the other was born, yet they are still linked together.

One of those people is me. I'm the latter. Born 116 years after the person I look to for inspiration. I get so much inspiration from Milton Hershey, who followed a path similar to my own. Perhaps that is what aligns us.

You may recognize the name. You might actually know him from the famous chocolate bar that you get at the best house in the neighborhood if you go trick-or-treating on Halloween. I sure do love those candy bars; however, I have a very different relationship with Milton Hershey than most people do. Here's why.

I learned about Milton Hershey in 1984. During the summer of 1984, I went to Hershey, Pennsylvania, to enroll in a private, tuition-free boarding school for disadvantaged children. At the time, my mom was a single parent raising three kids. The other two were causing quite a storm, so my mom tried to find a place for me that would have a bit more structure and keep me from behaving like my brothers. She found this school, located in Hershey, and it was a perfect fit. Why? Because it was free. It was created for people at or near the poverty line. The school provided food, clothing, and shelter—everything a kid would need. Enrolled in the school were kids of all ages, from kindergarteners to seniors in high school. They also provided a home-like atmosphere, where "house parents" (a married couple) would oversee a home with roughly sixteen boys or girls.

This school, at the time, had an enrollment of about 1,200. It was there, living in Hershey, that I started to understand who Milton Hershey was. At the age of ten, I started to look up to Mr. Hershey, but I was so young I had no concept of how much Hershey would change my life. Much of the inspiration, as it turns out, didn't appear until long after I graduated from high school in 1991.

As I ventured out on my own, success was just a fleeting thought. I was never really sure if I would be successful. I just knew I never wanted to be poor again. I started defining success as being able to pay my bills. In the '90s, I struggled greatly with this, teetering on the edge constantly. During that time, I learned what it's like to count the days before a check I wrote would be cashed, all in the hopes it would not bounce. This was before the debit card was the norm. Ultimately, it all crashed and burned, and I was bankrupt. In 1998, I made a pledge to myself that I would do everything in my power to never be poor again. Being poor was painful for me. It was a struggle to make ends meet. To this day, I sympathize with those who might be in that situation because it's very hard to break free from poverty. Living paycheck to paycheck isn't that much better. When I realized I had to focus on the right things to pull myself farther away from poverty, things started to turn around.

For me, it was not about being rich. I don't even truly know what it means to be rich since it's likely different for everyone. However, for me, striving for success meant putting distance between me and the poverty line every day. To this day, I still think about this. It drives me. I constantly tell myself, "I'm never going back there."

As I've grown older, though, I have realized that once our lives become stable, we can begin to focus on other things. I became more stable, more even-keeled. I started looking at Hershey's life, and I started drawing a few parallels between us. I saw his challenges and successes. I started to realize we had more in common than I ever would have imagined.

So why was it that I started looking up to Milton Hershey? Well, Hershey and his wife Katherine could not have children, so in 1909, Hershey put his fortune into a perpetual trust. The beneficiary of that trust (also known as The Deed of Trust) is the Milton Hershey School. Yep...that school. The one I attended.

At the time I enrolled at Milton Hershey School, I had *zero* idea who this Hershey guy was. I had no idea of the correlation between him, the chocolate company, and the school. Furthermore, for another twenty years, I had no idea about his business life.

As I grew older, I wanted to know more about Hershey. I wanted to know where he grew up, what his upbringing was like, his education, where he lived, but more so, I wanted to learn how he got into business and how he ran his businesses.

As it turns out, our business lives have had some similarities.

My business journey started when I volunteered to be a youth football coach. The association's board of directors needed a website, and I volunteered to head up the project. I had no idea what I was getting myself into. However, through pure grit and determination (something I learned at Milton Hershey School), I was able to pull the resources together and get the project done.

Soon after the website launched, Coach Morgan (from another team) hired me to design their association's website. With two websites under my belt, I launched a part-time digital marketing agency in the fall of 2002. This was the fourth business idea I had, and it was the one that finally stuck. In January 2005, I left my full-time cushy contracting job at Lycos.com and transitioned to fulltime in my digital marketing agency. I was taking a risk and a leap of faith, but I was confident in my ability to figure it out. Milton Hershey also took risks, numerous risks. That is a similarity that resonated with me. Both the chocolate dude and I were risk takers!

Milton Hershey himself came from a broken, single parent home. Neither one of us has a college degree. In fact, Milton Hershey only got as far as finishing the fourth grade! In my case. I'm the youngest of three boys, the first to graduate from high school, and the only one not to go to prison.

Milton Hershey believed in giving back to others, and I believe that's where my "give back" mentality comes from. Because money was often hard to come by, I gave my time. When I give to others, I feel great satisfaction, and that increases the value of the relationships I have with others. I know that, over time, others will be able to give back to me, or to someone else, and pay it forward. While I can't state this for a fact, I believe firmly that Milton Hershey had a similar mindset.

Another interesting parallel is the value we both see in relationships. Milton Hershey built relationships that mattered. He learned a great deal from other candy makers and specifically about caramels. He wasn't even twenty when he started his first caramel business using the knowledge he gained working for a Lancaster, Pennsylvania, caramel company.

While not everything Milton Hershey did turned to gold, he learned from his mistakes, and he continued to use his street smarts as he excelled in business. I've always said my best attribute is my ability to figure things out. I have no idea why—perhaps because I've considered myself independent and self-reliant for most of my life. At eighteen, after high school, I lived on my own, trying to figure out life. I do ask for advice when appropriate, and I believe in that; however, I feel my actions alone produce my results, and it's up to me to figure it out if I really want to get something done. Call it grit, determination, intestinal fortitude, or all three, but I know for sure I have these attributes. As I look at Milton Hershey's life, I see these attributes as well.

Neither Milton Hershey nor I just "ended up" business owners. We worked hard, using grit and determination, to find the right fit in clients, partners, and business models for us. We did it in our own way, with others' help and by building on the relationships we cultivated, to create a better life for ourselves and those around us.

I wrote this book with the hope that I might be able to help other small business owners move from a business that creates anxiety and controls them to a more fulfilling business that includes more Joy.

This book is **not** for you if:

- You're currently happy with the way your business is running.
- You don't have any concerns or anxiety over the clients you have.
- You don't see a ton of value in relationships.
- You don't have a service-based business.

If one of the above describes you, then while you certainly may get something from the book, and even implement a few tips, please understand that this book is focused on creating a service business that brings you joy.

This book is for you if:

- You own or operate a service-based business, and you would like it to run more smoothly.
- You are anxious or concerned about your clients.
- You don't feel your business makes enough money.
- You don't feel you have enough time outside of your business.
- You don't feel free to do what you want, when you want, because you're tied to the business.
- You believe (at least somewhat) that relationships are the core of your business.

I invite you to come along on this journey with me. In the first chapter, we will define for you what Joy is as it relates to a business. What it means for you and why it matters so much. I'm deeply passionate about helping service-based business owners build a business that eliminates the anxiety most of us have or had at one point. Ready? Let's go!

*"Grit and determination get you through the work every day, but it's the people on both sides of the table who make everything worth it. And, it's the clients and partners you can "high-five" who make the work more fun, who contribute to higher profits, and who fill our professional and personal lives with joy."*

— Matt Ward

# INTRODUCTION TO BUSINESS *JOY*

*"People do business with those they know,*

*like, trust, and care about."*

— Matt Ward

---

# CHAPTER 1

# DEFINING *JOY*

**Why Do We Want to Own Our Own Business?**

Many people who own a business do so to acquire more money, more time, and more freedom. At the beginning, we are overwhelmed with joy because it is new and exciting, and we are going to "rule the world." Then, it feels a little more like "real work." Struggles start creeping in. We find ourselves working with good clients and not-so-good clients. At this point, we only feel joy intermittently, and it decreases month by month because we realize that no matter how hard we work, the profits are not what we expected. Frustration begins to set in, and we ask ourselves, "How do I get out of this spiral and make this business work like it should? I don't love this life at all."

The answer lies in understanding why we got into the business we are in. What's that thing that brought us to the point of owning our own business? It's about finding the joy in that, and then figuring out how to keep it that way. This is how I think of it...

*"What I really want is to work with clients I can share a drink with and high-five. That would bring me back to my joy on day one."*

*— Matt Ward*

I'm completely aware that joy may mean something different to everyone in business. I even know quite a few people who would never actually want to high-five someone. For them, it's just awkward. That's why I feel it's important to define for you what I believe joy is, as well as what I mean by a high-five. It's also deeply important to me that you take a few minutes to define what joy means to you in your business.

Running a business has so many facets, from client acquisition to employee management. Of course, there are too many items to list, many of which used to cause me anxiety or even small, short heart palpitations. When I went into business back in 2002, I just wanted to help people solve a problem. Little did I know doing so would create other problems. Those problems robbed me of my joy.

As I took a hard look at my life and my business, I quickly realized I wanted much more. To me, business wasn't just a transaction. In fact, the relationships I gained from business are what inspired me to continue on. Relationships were my financial capital. This desire for those relationships may partially stem from my upbringing; however, where they come from was, and still is, irrelevant to me. There's something about creating, building, and maintaining relationships with people that drives me to be who I am today. Yes, there is much more to a business, including sales. I know that if I don't sell my product or service, I ultimately have no business and I'll be on the street with nothing but a boatload of relationships. The good news is, those relationships are capital as well; they just don't pay the mortgage! Sadly, I can't exchange them for cash and pay my mortgage; if I could, I'd have hundreds of homes!

So...what is my definition of joy? For me, it comes down to one word, which I will talk a lot about in this book: freedom.

What I found throughout my time running multiple businesses is that I became less passionate about what I was doing, and for whom I was doing it for, if my decisions were led by something other than freedom. To me, freedom is the ability to do:

- what I want
- when I want
- where I want, and
- how I want.

Now, to be very clear, I can't achieve any of that without the right business model, the right products and services, and certainly the right clients. When I did not have those things, freedom was not there, and as a result, I had less joy in my business and life. With great relationships, both with clients and with others, I can increase the level of joy and the likelihood of more freedom.

Take a moment to define what joy means to you. Consider a few questions to help you create your own definition.

Questions to ask yourself:

- What makes me happy?
- What types of things make me smile?
- Do people in general make me happy?
- If so, what individual, personally or professionally, do I enjoy having in my presence?
- If no, then in the absence of people, what makes me happy?

Now that you have defined what joy is for you, keep that definition in your mind. We'll come back to it in later chapters, but just know that achieving the reality of your definition of joy is our goal here.

I believe relationships are the core of a joyous, successful, service-based small business, no matter how you define that relationship with your contacts and clients. If that is true, and you also can embrace this idea, then this book is for you, and it may, in fact, reframe how you run your business.

If, by chance, people and relationships are not near the top of this list for you, then this book might not be for you. If that is the case and you've already bought this book, email me a copy of your receipt and I will refund you the price you paid for the book. I only ask that you give the book to another business owner as a gift so they may possibly benefit.

### How Does Your Business Make You Feel?

### vs.

### How Do You Want to Feel?

We all have a way to describe the feelings our business brings us or the feelings we want our business to bring us. Look through the list and think about and/or circle both the positive and negative feelings you have about your business today.

## HOW DO I FEEL ABOUT MY BUSINESS TODAY?

| Positive | Negative |
|---|---|
| Comfortable | Okay |
| Delightful | Frustrated |
| Gleeful | Serious |
| Proud | Discouraged |
| Satisfied | Hateful |
| Festive | Regretful |
| Glad | Rejected |
| Jubilant | Depressed |
| Happy | Angry |
| Contented | Shocked |
| Fulfilled | Aggravated |
| Joyful | Miserable |

Chances are you have a mix of both types of feelings at any given time during any given day. That's normal. If you have more negatives than positives circled, that's an indication to assess what has happened since day one. You can then determine how you would like to swing the pendulum to revisit the purpose you set when you launched your business.

Throughout my twenty-five-plus years of working for others and then for myself, I've learned some painful lessons. The positive aspect of pain-evoking lessons is that we *actually* learn from them. When we recognize them, and when we take action on them, we shift the paradigm to avoid repeating them. We also learn what we do well throughout building a business, and then, hopefully, we incorporate more of the good.

I've also learned, over time, that building a successful business requires sharing key insights with others. I share what's working well for me with colleagues and they do the same. That allows me to improve my company with their ideas, and it allows me to pay it forward to others and help them grow. The legacy of building community and giving to others, which Milton Hershey passes on through the education of the students at Milton Hershey School, holds strong to the values I hold within both my professional and personal lives.

I'll never forget that day in 2005 when I went full-time in my business. I knew I wanted more from life. I knew I wanted...

**MORE MONEY, MORE TIME, AND MORE FREEDOM**

# CHAPTER 2

# THE BUSINESS OWNER'S EVOLUTION OF *JOY*

"Yeah, baby. I have a new business!" Nothing is more joyful than the moment we announce to everyone we know that we have our own business. "I only report to *me*." Owning a business has a lot going for it. After all, the elusive enterprise of entrepreneurship is said to give us more money, more time, and more freedom. That's why we do this, right?

According to the Small Business Association (SBA), 20 percent of all businesses fail within the first year.[1] If we last five years, we are considered a great success. Say what?

When we open our business, we don't plan to fail in the first, fifth, tenth, or twentieth year. I don't know about you, but when I opened my business, I wondered how it could be so difficult to keep a business alive for five years. Now that I've owned, operated, and sold businesses since 2002, I have seen the good, the bad, and the ugly of entrepreneurship. As the months and years ticked by, I found myself wanting more than money, time, and freedom. I, personally, yearned to find *joy* in, around, and throughout my business and personal life. I

---

1 Small Business Association, https://www.sba.gov/sites/default/files/Business-Survival.pdf

figured if I had to work so hard, I might as well enjoy it through all the phases of business ownership.

When I started, days rolled into each other. Weeks started feeling like ten days. Sometimes I really didn't know what day it was because it was all melting together. I got to the point where if I was asked what day it was, I'd answer with "Blursday." This, in hindsight, was one red flag I should have kept an eye on.

As owners, we get to choose how we want to conduct our business. Through my experience working with hundreds of small business owners and the dozens of interviews I conducted for this book, I've learned so much about the importance of the *joy* we experience when we build relationships with our clients. When we work together, we build trust, receive value, share respect, and achieve our goals. In this way, we benefit mutually from the relationships, and we both find the experience enjoyable and rewarding.

Interestingly enough, in relationship-driven businesses we find that seeking *joy* in our business relationships leads to earning more money, having more time, and yes, having more freedom.

However, it was not easy to realize this "secret of all secrets." I believe good things come to those who work hard, learn from their mistakes, and desire better outcomes. This, I believe, ultimately helps people achieve higher goals and dreams.

It took me a long time to figure this out.

Too long.

Now that I have, I want to save business owners like you the time, money, and mistakes I made. Why? So that we can crush the one-year failure rate of new businesses and help you find joy a lot sooner and with a lot less pain. Let's start healing our wounds, broken bones, and heartaches from the sucky part of business and set our path on finding *joy*.

Change is required to achieve great outcomes. That means we need to evolve. I call this process:

## THE BUSINESS OWNERS' EVOLUTION OF JOY

You will move through five phases on your business journey. These are phases of growth that ultimately attract *joy* to your business, which also translates to joy in your personal life. Let's dig into these briefly. Let's start with the smallest circle and end with the biggest one.

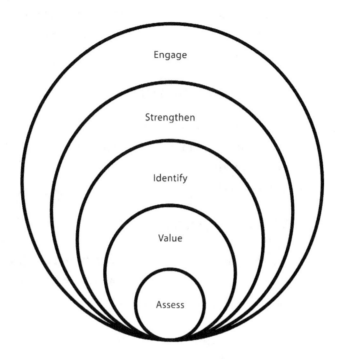

Business Owners' Evolution of Joy

## ASSESS

First, we need to **assess** where we are in our business. What are we trying to achieve? What do we want more of? What do we want less of? What do we need to do to make that happen?

## VALUE

Second, how do we **value** ourselves, our business, our expertise, our services, and other people, including our clients? Do we want those perceptions to change? Are we providing enough value for others and accurately recognizing the value we provide?

## IDENTIFY

Then, we take time to **identify** the changes we want to make to drastically improve our business. Those improvements will help us realize our goal of making more money, and having the time and freedom entrepreneurship promises.

## STRENGTHEN

The strongest will survive, and business fitness is a must in building the business we desire from this point forward. When we **strengthen** key areas for those we serve, the core of our business becomes the strongest foundation for survival.

## ENGAGE

And then, with all this hard and worthwhile work completed, we will **engage** in great relationships with the people we can serve best. This is when we are rewarded with more money, more time, and more freedom.

In fact, instead of whistling a happy tune, you'll be grabbing a frosty adult beverage with your clients and business friends while you high-five them in celebration of your great successes throughout the years.

In this book, I will walk you through The High-Five Effect, and you will learn how to integrate the Five Phases of building a business with clients you know, like, trust, *and* care about. These are the clients you can grab a beer with and experience *joy* with when you *high-five* them—or whatever your metaphorical high-five is.

From your *business' perspective*, think about and document your answers (if you wish) to the following questions about where you are today. This great exercise will help guide you in identifying which phase of the process you are currently in.

Keep in mind that, as you evolve as a business, you may move into the next phase. However, sometimes we fall back just a bit, and that may mean moving back to the previous phase.

## ASSESS

- ❏ Where are you today?
- ❏ Where do you wish you were?
- ❏ Who are your clients?

## VALUE

- ❏ How do you value yourself (as in experience, expertise, skill set)?
- ❏ How do you value your business (as in your products and/or services)?
- ❏ What type of value do you place on your pricing? Do you believe your pricing is fair compared to the market, your competitors, the value you bring, and the services you offer?

## IDENTIFY

- ❏ What do you really want for yourself, your professional life, and personal life? What is missing? What is fabulous?
- ❏ What do you really want for your business? Which changes do you want to make? What is broken? What is working well?
- ❏ Do you want to provide more value, services, products, processes, or relationships?

## STRENGTHEN

- ❏ Do you want/need to strengthen your business operations and decision making?
- ❏ Do you desire to strengthen your position in the community or industry?
- ❏ Do you need to define your filters or processes when making decisions, such as picking best-fit clients?

## ENGAGE

- ❏ Would you like clients who are better aligned with your business philosophy?
- ❏ Would you like to offload clients who siphon *joy* from your business?
- ❏ Would you like to surround yourself with clients who bring you *joy*?

Once you get through this exercise, we will unpack each step in "The Business Owners Evolution of *Joy*" and introduce you to The High-Five Effect.

# CHAPTER 3

# HOW DID WE GET HERE?

After walking through the short exercise at the end of Chapter 2 to ask yourself questions about your business, you may have discovered some interesting insights. For me, what stood out most when I started asking those questions years ago was the shocking thought, *How on earth did I get here? How did I get to this point?* That's something I think is important to explore, not only as individuals but collectively as business owners.

I believe business owners get frustrated because they don't focus on the right things. Furthermore, I think the misaligned focus stems from the fact that many small business owners don't know what they don't know.

We only have so much time in the day, and we are doing the best we can with what we have. Most focus on sales for survival and end up putting short-term things first, rather than focusing on some of the most important things.

So...how did we get here?

The Answer: Collectively!

We got here together. We did what everyone else did, and that's why so many people are unhappy in their small businesses. It's why they struggle day in and day out.

It's time for change.

So...

## DO YOU WANT MORE?

Desiring better results is always the catalyst for change. Call it a paradigm shift, swinging the pendulum, or whatever you wish. The desire is deep, and a shift of great proportions is usually necessary to achieve the desired outcome. You picked up this book, so you, too, are looking for change. What is the outcome you most desire in your professional or personal life?

Many people want to know that their life *means* something, that they have a purpose. We do, and it's our job to discover it. More often than not, the end result is something we want to *feel*. Return to the positive words list in Chapter 1 and pick the word that most resonates with you as you look to make your life more meaningful.

Do we wish owning a business was much easier and success happened on its own? Of course, but we know that's not the case. Wouldn't it be nice if we could plan it all out before we start and have everything work the way we envisioned? But most of the time, we evolve. Our expectations of business evolution aren't generally in line with how often we must evolve. We must evolve; we are human. Yes, it seems as though for some "everything goes their way." Oh, how lucky they are. For most of us, building a business takes hard work, dedication, and persistence. Besides, do we really know the lucky one's struggles? No, we don't. Suffice it to say, they most likely have some struggles, but they are not apparent to us. We just think they have it easy because we don't *see* them struggle.

Fortunately, changes in business do not take as long as it took to turn a T-rex into a pigeon. It may feel like it in some circumstances, but with this book as your guide, your evolution is well on its way, and it will not take eons for you to achieve...

MORE MONEY, MORE TIME, MORE FREEDOM,

AND ULTIMATELY, MORE *JOY*!

---

# CHAPTER 4

# CLIENTS WE'VE ENCOUNTERED

As time went on, I found my *joy* in the great relationships I had with clients. Service-based businesses rely on relational experiences with clients rather than transactional. Purchasing gas for the car is transactional. You fill up, pay, and leave. You buy gas at a given station primarily based on location. It's rarely about how you feel about the station clerk.

Partnering with a digital marketing agency can be either transactional or relational. If all communication between client and provider is short and to the point, it's a transactional relationship. If you also talk about business in general, plans, hopes, and aspirations, etc., then it is a relationship.

Do you see the difference between a relationship and a transaction?

Coffee at the drive-thru every day with nothing more than pleasantries (good morning, thank you, etc.) is a transaction.

Ordering coffee every day with, "How is your mother recovering from the procedure?" is a relationship.

Some people just want their coffee. Others want the conversation and the relationship. Ultimately, everyone is different when it comes to these interactions, so it's a sliding scale for sure.

Additionally, as I found out over time, my clients would fall into certain previously undefined categories. As I started researching this book, I listed some clients and tried to put them into categories. I refer to these categories as client types. The four client types I've defined are:

- **Adequate Clients**
- **Challenging Clients**
- **Risky Clients**
- **Great Clients**

Before we get started, remember, these are general attributes we will use to help identify common client needs and characteristics. They are useful as long as we remember we are dealing with individuals and no two people are exactly alike.

Let's take a look at these categories one by one at a high level to help define them. Later, we'll dig into them deeply to gain clarity about "standard" client behaviors. It's important to understand the makeup of these client types because they control so much of our business, including the relationships we have with them, our thoughts, and ultimately, our *joy*.

**Adequate Clients** are generally transaction-driven. Even though they are not necessarily the customers who want to know much about you, you probably like working with them because they are cool, easy to work for, and often come back for more. Adequate clients don't generally cause problems and rarely take up extra time outside of the actual transaction.

**Challenging Clients** are transaction-driven people who tend to be frustrating to work with for multiple reasons. They might:

- waste our time
- pay late
- use questionable ethics
- disrespect or devalue our work
- disrespect our processes
- ask for more work for less money

I consider these challenging clients because they take too much of our time, make things difficult, and rarely result in a profit.

**Risky Clients** tend to be relationship-driven and often love having relationships with their vendors, like you. They enjoy building the relationships, which is great, but that also can take a ton of time. While that's what we are looking for as a service-based business, it falls short when they don't really have the resources to pay for what they want/need or just want someone to talk to. I consider them risky because they can take a lot of your time and leave you drained without making a profit in the process.

**Great Clients** are relationship-driven. It is very satisfying to work with them because they are pleasant, praise you for what you do well, and pay their bills on time. They ask about your family and your social life. They are nice people, and you like to be around them. I call these clients great because they bring you *joy*.

You'll certainly have a mix of all of these clients, and you will likely have a client who doesn't fit into any of these four categories. But I think you will find a place for all your clients inside the Ideal Client Matrix.

### IDEAL CLIENT MATRIX

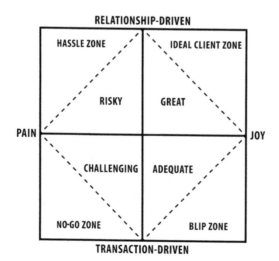

Later, I'll show you how to use this client matrix to plot your clients and how to move them from one section to another.

# CHAPTER 5

# THE BUSINESS OWNER'S JOURNEY TO *JOY*

Making your business joyful is a journey. It's not something you can do overnight or at the snap of your fingers. Furthermore, you didn't get where you are overnight. It was a long process. It will be work to climb back up. What we are going to do is start the process of reimagining the *joy* you want from your business; then we will take action to ensure we start to replace the clients who steal our joy by attracting and keeping ones who bring *joy*.

In Chapter 2, I talked about the business owner's evolution of *joy* and the phases that a business owner goes through. I just want to take a moment to reiterate that evolution takes time. Be patient; this works.

The moment you start questioning if this process works is the moment you need to change your thinking and be patient, looking more toward the future goal of joy and away from negative thoughts. The best thing you can do if this thought pops into your head is to take action. In subsequent chapters, I'll give you some action you can take that will move you closer to *joy*. When you take action, your focus will be on that action and not on the thoughts and questions about the process.

**ARE YOU READY TO ASSESS YOUR BUSINESS?**

**LET'S GO!**

# PHASE I

# CHAPTER 6

---

# THE CLIENT ACQUISITION HIERARCHY OF NEEDS

You *can* handle the truth. You picked up this book, which means you are ready to get your business exactly where you want it and exactly where you need it. The first step is to Assess. In this phase, you will evaluate, examine, review, and analyze the functions of your business. Then, you'll know more about what's working and what's not, so you can do more of what is working.

What is it that you are trying to achieve? Where do you struggle? Which path do you want to travel? I guarantee, I, and every business owner I've met in the past twenty years, have experienced most of your struggles. While you may think you're unique, or even an anomaly, you are, in fact, not; *you are not alone.*

Business is difficult and exhilarating on any given day, month, or year. Some people are better at camouflaging their challenges and some wear them like badges of honor. "Fake it 'til you make it" and "I will survive" are mantras we play in our head on repeat to get through the tough times and drive ourselves to crazy town—I mean, success. As long as you are not stuck believing the whole world is against you, you are ready to evolve your business into one that brings you joy.

One of the most interesting discoveries I've made as a business owner was realizing that so many others in my position felt the same way I did. For so long, I thought I was the only one struggling with client acquisition, employee management, and business success. I learned through deep meaningful discussions with other business owners that we all share the same issues. We are all playing the same game; we just have different players.

My first business was a digital marketing agency that I sold in 2018 for seven figures. Today, I'm a speaker, author, referral consultant, and franchise owner. Generally speaking, I interact with at least 200 business owners per week, and I repeatedly hear the same frustrations with their businesses. Many people struggle with various areas of their business. It is painful to deal with people who are not fun to work with. Often, in the first couple of years, business owners take on clients without knowing if the client is a good fit, and it often leads the business owner down a rough road. I get frustrated for them. It drives me crazy.

Challenges we have had, are having, or will have are common across all businesses. What has been your greatest struggle as a business owner? Which challenges are you currently experiencing?

Thinking back to my days with my agency, I fondly recall the work we did for Toys for Tots. We nurtured our relationship with them over the course of three years, with great returns for them and pleasing revenue for us. At the peak of our work with them, we managed forty-five different websites in many major cities and regions in the USA. The various Toy for Tots locations were incredibly pleased with our services. Those were the exhilarating days of business ownership. In this case, our clients were the coordinators for Toys for Tots in each city, and they referred their counterparts and colleagues all over the country to us!

Working together, we were able to serve more kids and really make a difference in many communities. It was a win-win. As my agency grew, we desired a long-term relationship with Toys for Tots. We carefully listened as they described new features that would streamline the user experience on their websites. We invested in expanding the product so we would be ready to roll when Toys for Tots started their new season on October 1. Then, on September 1, Toy for Tots notified us that the home office had made a global decision—beginning immediately, no coordinator, at any site in the US, could use outside web providers. Our investment in the product was wasted, and our invoices, which were about to go out, would not be paid. We lost forty-five clients in one day—probably the most difficult day in business for me. We had invested time, resources, and money into something that so many people found valuable. Unfortunately, things changed, and boom, it was all gone. Tough day. Really tough day.

This is just one of the memorable challenges I faced owning a business. I'm certain you've lost that whale client too, or maybe it's another challenge of epic proportions that set you back and made you rethink your relationship with your clients or even your business as a whole. Perhaps you lost clients during the 2020 pandemic. Whatever it was, just know that you aren't alone in this process. While your specific situation might be unique to you, it's very similar to the situation the person sitting next to you at a conference had last month or is even going through today.

## YOU'VE OPENED YOUR BUSINESS! NOW WHAT?

When we open our businesses, we feel *joy*. We love telling everyone we know, "I have my own business now!" Do you remember that day? Do you remember how excited you were? I remember that excitement. Even though others couldn't, we clearly saw our vision as a path to more money, more time, and more freedom. Of course, we assumed it was going to happen automatically. "Print the business card, launch the website, and immediately, the phone will ring. I'll break the internet with inbound emails and..." Ha! If it were only that easy.

When I sold the agency, I sat back and assessed what went right and what went wrong. I unpacked a lot of lessons, and it stung. That was painful, which is a good sign. It's not that I didn't have great times with the agency. I did. Some of the things I looked back on stung, and some of them made me feel like a rock star. However, pain is where we learn our greatest lessons and how we are motivated to change. I realized I had offered too many services and the work itself didn't bring me joy. In fact, it brought me pain. I also realized I gravitated toward working with the people who were fun and gave me joy. I promised myself that any future business endeavor would focus solely on building a business filled with clients, business partners, and referral sources who brought me more joy!

It's time to evolve. Let's assess the state of your business and look at ways we can improve it. But first, remember three things:

- You *can* handle the truth.
- Be *honest* with yourself.
- It might sting a bit. You are going for *joy*. To get there, you might first have to feel a little pain.

## ASSESS YOUR BUSINESS

The following questions are for your review and consideration. You are welcome to answer these now or later if you wish. Here's the scale to use when rating yourself on the questions:

1 – No Joy
2 – I'm Not Failing, Yet
3 – Decent
4 – Good
5 – Great & Joyful

_____ On a scale of one to five, where do you rate your business?
_____ Are you happy with your clients? Do you want to keep them?
_____ Are you frustrated with your clients?
_____ How much joy do you experience in your business?

Here are other great questions to ask yourself...

Would you like to see some of your clients move on?

What have you learned through this evaluation?

Using the same scale above, how do you feel now?

My first book was published in 2018 when I became a professional speaker, *MORE...: Word of Mouth Referrals, Lifelong Customers & Raving Fans*. *MORE* includes forty-five lessons and tips for building deeper, more meaningful relationships with others. These are relationships that can last a lifetime if we stay in touch and engaged.

The secret of *MORE* is to build your business with contacts and clients you *care* about. It sounds easy enough, right? But in practice, the philosophy is much more developed than simply "caring" about some-one. As I developed the "caring" message, I remembered a commonly known rule for working with clients and hiring people—choose to work with and hang around people you "know, like, and trust." To me, though, this "rule" as defined is not enough. Instead, the rule I've come to strongly believe in is to choose people "I know, like, trust, and *care* about." It's a small, single word change, but it's powerful.

Care...this sweet little four-letter word has become the compass guiding my decisions on the clients with whom I choose to engage. This is no simple feat, and it took me a long, long time to figure it out. I really hope this book will help to tremendously shorten your learning curve and alleviate a lot of pain. None of us should struggle as much as we do to be successful in business.

## A BUSINESS' NEEDS ARE NO LONGER A MYSTERY— IT'S ALL ABOUT CLIENTS

In 1943, Abraham Harold Maslow published a paper, "A Theory of Human Motivation," in the journal *Psychological Review*. In his paper, Maslow presented his hierarchy of needs, which described the pattern that human motivations generally follow. He said that to move through the stages, people had to be satisfied within each preceding stage. Maslow used a five-stage, pyramid-shaped diagram to illustrate the hierarchy of human needs:

1. Physiological Needs
2. Safety Needs
3. Love and Belongingness Needs
4. Esteem Needs
5. Self-Actualization Needs

This model has been used to represent pretty much everything in the world from psychology, therapy, business, e-learning, and employee motivation to culture and now **clients**. For owners seeking *joy* in their business through the work they do and whom they do it with, I present a new rendition of Maslow's model, "The Client Acquisition Hierarchy of Needs."

# CLIENT ACQUISITION
# HIERARCHY OF NEEDS

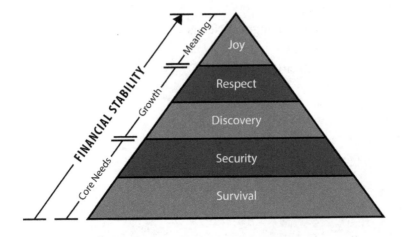

Download A Printable Version Here: https://bit.ly/
ClientAcquisitionHierarchyOfNeeds

During our years as business owners, we go through five stages of business maturation. In each of these stages, based on our experience and degree of success, we say, do, think, or feel certain universal things. As we mature as owners, we learn lessons nearly every day about the business and our relationships with prospective clients and clients who have said "yes!" to us. As we graduate from each stage, we learn how to shift, pivot, and change. Some of us who stay in the lower stages too long may never graduate to the next level. In that case, it might be too hard to sustain the business, and we may need to close the doors. It's been that way for me at times. I've started several different business ventures, both alone and with partners. Not all of them have succeeded. In some cases, I was that SBA statistic I mentioned earlier (one in five businesses fail in the first five years), and you know what—it sucked.

It's my mission, through this book, to encourage as many business owners as I can so we don't have to struggle. The sooner we understand our needs as they relate to client relationships, the sooner we gain more money, more time, more freedom, *and* experience *joy*.

## IT'S TIME TO EVOLVE FROM PRIMAL INSTINCT TO PURE HAPPINESS

In researching this book, I was extremely fortunate to interview fifty business owners about their own experiences. Kathy Fisher, co-owner at Fisher Green Creative in Maine, said most of her mistakes happened early on. Fisher recognized she "had a hunch" about certain people whom she took on as clients. After working with them for a while, she realized her hunch was warning her they may not be a "good fit."

"When we are new to business, we want the business, and we want the assurance of a steady stream of income, so we take on any client," explains Fisher. Acquiring clients is the most important aspect of a business. Without them, there is no business.

In those formidable years, like most business owners, Fisher was focused on survival, which is a primal instinct. She took on a client, even though she had a hunch they might not be ideal because she wanted her business to grow and, quite frankly, survive. As you might expect, it didn't work out well.

Her best client turned out to be Dr. A, a dentist. Fisher immediately felt comfortable with Dr. A and had no negative hunches about working with him. As we talked about Dr. A, I could see Fisher's body language change drastically. Clearly, working with Dr. A brings her and her business partner, Jenny, joy. Fisher said, "Jenny and I have talked about how we would love a few more clients like Dr. A."

Who wouldn't?

**That's what this book is all about**—identifying the clients who bring you *joy*.

In the interviews I conducted with business owners, as we went from talking about worst to best clients, each interviewee's body language shifted as if on cue. The first few years in business are about survival; we are building business acumen, refining our services, and learning how to deal with people. In this lean phase, we say yes to every client who chooses us because we don't know what we don't know.

It's difficult to be discerning about who we work with because, again, for a business to grow and survive, we need the clients, and our primal instinct tells us to take on every one of them. Fortunately, as our business grows, our self-talk, self-esteem, confidence, understanding, and capacity to discern good from bad fits matures through each of the stages of the client acquisition hierarchy of needs. We discover it is important that our client acquisition process and goals evolve.

As we graduate each level, our client list and acquisition processes must change to allow for more growth, more income, more ease, and more *joy*!

# CHAPTER 7

# SURVIVAL STAGE

Quick Assessment—How do I know if I'm in the Survival Stage?

**Do you say, do, think, or feel any of the following?**

| SAY | DO | THINK | FEEL |
|---|---|---|---|
| • Yeah, baby new business!<br><br>• I need sales.<br><br>• Yes, yes, yes! To all clients.<br><br>• I need money. | • Work late nights and weekends.<br><br>• Take on more clients, any clients, any heartbeat.<br><br>• Struggle.<br><br>• Give up self-care family, friends, vacations, time off. | • Is this what owning a business it?<br><br>• Profits? How?<br><br>• How am I going to pay the bills?<br><br>• I'm desparate for money. | • Excited.<br><br>• Frustrated.<br><br>• Overwhelmed.<br><br>• Exhausted.<br><br>• Sad.<br><br>• Disappointed. |

## STAGE SUMMARY

If you find yourself aligning with any of the thoughts and feelings listed in the chart, then you are likely in the Survival Stage. Generally speaking, this is where most early-stage business owners find themselves. In this stage, you say, do, think, and feel these things early on.

If this is not where you are, it's probably okay to jump ahead to the next stage. However, don't blame me if you miss a good story about some fish.

---

As new business owners, we do everything possible to attract clients so we can pay for food, shelter, clothing, and keep the lights on. It's in our nature. We hunt and gather to cover our basic needs. It's a primal instinct. Eons ago, early humans hunted and gathered to provide for their families. When it comes to operating a business, we often take the "I need money now" approach. That is instinctual, and yet, it causes us to look at a woolly mammoth and say, "I can take that down." In other words, we make decisions that make our job even harder and sometimes even make our business unbearable.

With a new business comes advice, opinions, and "squirrels" from every direction. As we are trying to juggle 100 balls, we hear from all directions:

- "You need a business plan."
- "Identify your target market and stay there."
- "What's your niche? Pick your lane and stay there!"
- "Create a buyer persona."
- "You need to work more on your business than in your business."

The advice goes on, and on, and on. And we say to ourselves:

- "Yes, yes, yes. I will work with you. Oh, you need a fat discount? Okay!"
- "Maybe I should try this—oh, this is better—oh, here's another idea!"
- "Yes, I can offer you all of that and a jumbo bag of chips!"
- "Oh, my gosh, when was the last day I had off?"
- "What is wrong with me? I can get along with everyone else, but this specific client."

And you go on, and on, and on like this.

We don't know where to listen, how to say no, or when we should say yes, so we muddle through building a business, figuring it out with piecemeal advice from our friends or other business owners and our own instincts.

Remember that business plan everyone said you had to have? Forget about it. It's now kindling for the backyard fire. We don't have that kind of time. And we are not asking banks to give us money. Besides, in our fast-paced society, the new approach to business (since the tech ages) is "we're up and running." There's no time for a business plan.

If as a business owner you are a planner who likes to map everything out, just remember that the traditional business plan is designed to submit proposals to banks and investors for funding. If that is not a route you see in your future, modify your plan to include the necessary information that will keep you on track. It doesn't have to be perfect, and you can do a little at a time over time. Don't sweat it. Personally, I'm not convinced that a business plan makes or breaks the business. If you feel it will help you map out a strategy for your business, then fine, put something down on paper. I rarely, if ever, had a business plan, and I did just fine establishing and growing my businesses. I managed to keep all the balls in the air, rarely ever dropping one.

In reality, what you need is to surround yourself with a few great business owners whom you respect and trust. Bounce ideas of these folks and get their feedback. Do not take advice from every business owner out there because that will result in the wild, wild west of business ownership. You might end up taking advice from failing business owners. Do your homework. Surround yourself with great people.

Juggling all the bits and pieces of a new business is no easy task. Owners find it exceedingly difficult to do the work, develop new business, and follow up with prospects. Doing the actual work completely consumes the day since it is the top priority. Instead, delegating work should be a main objective, so you, the business owner, can work on building the business by creating new offerings, managing staff, designing processes, and developing new client relationships. If you want to really dig into this issue and switch to working on your business, pick up *The E-Myth Revisited* by Michael Gerber. This book completely altered my thinking about running a business, putting me in the right place to continue to grow my business.

I knew nothing about the jargon of entrepreneurship when I started. I didn't know what any of the made-up, twisted, redefined, and mangled English meant. I didn't know how to find the right market—and I certainly didn't know what an avatar was. All I wanted to do was build websites for people who wanted them—people who came to me. I thought I could just sit back and catch the business coming my way. But then...clients weren't just coming my way. I never realized how long it would take for businesses in my community to find me or even know my company existed.

As business owners, we worry incessantly about when, where, and how we will get our next client. The minute we open our doors, we are willing to take anyone who walks in. It's like your business has a Tinder profile and everyone is swiping right.

Because we worry so much, and in an effort to get as many clients as we can, we ignore expert advice to identify the "ideal client persona" and instead opt for casting a wide net to catch as many fish as we can. Without knowing our "ideal client," we say yes to every client who says yes to us. This isn't very effective, which is a tough lesson for a new business owner.

When I spoke to Nicole Porter from Monomoy Social Media, a small social media management company located on Cape Cod, she said, "At the beginning, I worried about getting new clients very much." She also told me she took on any client willing to sign her agreement and pay her.

The problem was Porter was looking for clients everywhere, casting a wide net—she was after any or all the fish in the ocean, and she took whatever she could catch. She was not shooting fish in a barrel. What I mean by "shooting fish in a barrel" is defining your client base and understanding who you are selling to. This limits the number of fish you are after and rounds them up, putting them in a metaphorical barrel so you can focus on clients who fit your offerings and style.

Many business owners, including myself, look back and regret not limiting their focus to the clients who best fit their services. We see how taking on all clients resulted in a painful business life. We can also see how finding our niche and defining our target market was the beginning of tremendous growth. At that point, we kick ourselves for ignoring the advice to define what we are fishing for and limiting our catch to the barrel we build around that definition.

When I spoke to Amanda Macinnes from Primerica Insurance, she was just getting started in business. I asked her if she ever wonders about where her next client will come from. "Yes, I do worry about that; however, I don't focus on the worry. I don't allow the worry to control my actions in a negative way. The worry actually drives me to solve the worry."

Macinnes went on to say something I find very profound, especially for someone so new to owning a business: "My worry drives my want and my need to be successful!"

When you ask a business owner whom they serve, whom their ideal client is, or whom you can refer to them, the most common response is, "I can help everyone in any industry needing anything I offer. Oh, and I'll customize and extend my services to meet their needs. I don't want to limit my services to a small, target market." This is referred to in marketing as casting a wide net or the shotgun approach.

Picture going to a networking event as a graphic designer who believes you can help everyone. Yes, you probably can, but soon you find the people you are networking with do not have the budget to pay for your services. Instead of catching a high-end, quality fish like salmon in your barrel, you caught minnows in a net you thought would hold them, but all the minnows fell through the holes. So, you go get a net with smaller holes. You cast that net and pull out more minnows. Great job!

Or maybe not. Sure, you can likely help these minnows, but you lose money on them, so why do it? You are in business to *make money*. Don't forget that. The time you spend working with minnows could be spent working with the salmon who has funds and knows other salmon who need your services *and* also have funds. Do you want more minnows or salmon? This is exactly why identifying your target market and creating a buyer profile is important. We can't serve all the business people out there. Be patient in identifying your target market, and you'll find that you're serving the right market for you. This focus alone will help bring more joy to your business.

Fortunately, as we mature as business owners, we learn that casting a wide net and taking on all comers is/was not a good strategy. The experts (and even business owners who have come before us and given us advice) really do know their stuff. If we try to serve everyone and anyone, we serve none well, make less money, and lose some of the enthusiasm that helped us start our own business in the first place. Instead, we should define our ideal clients (called "creating a client persona" in marketing circles where plain English is frowned upon) so we can focus on the clients who will bring us more revenue and more joy.

The idiom "shooting fish in a barrel" comes from the time when fish were packed in barrels with ice for shipment. The barrels were jam-packed with fish. If you shot into the barrel, you would hit at least one fish—as opposed to trying to shoot a fish in the wild, where the likelihood of hitting it was slim. Rounding up a select group of prospects makes securing clients quite easy.

*"Give someone a fish and you feed them for a day.*

*Teach them to round up fish and dump them into a barrel and you feed them for a lifetime.*

*Or at least until the barrel is empty!"*

*— Matt Ward*

I spoke to Ronii Bartles about buyer personas, or client avatars, if you prefer, and their relevance in small business. Bartles is a marketing consultant who specializes in creating buyer personas for her clients. She said:

> Creating buyer personas for your business is important because it helps you get clarity, focus, and save money. When you take the time to really understand who your perfect customer is from demographics to psychographics, everything in your business becomes clear. You get clear on what you do and can focus on your zone of genius. And your customer is clear on exactly what you offer so it's easy for them to buy your product or service.

That clarity and focus saves you money and time on everything because you don't need to chase all the shiny objects in hopes that it'll be the magic pill that finally makes you money.

What's clear to me is buyer personas create clarity and help us attract customers to us rather than us chasing customers, which, frankly, makes us look desperate.

## ROTTING FISH LEAVE A BAD TASTE

"I got one!"

The absolute excitement of landing a new client creates a euphoric moment for a small business owner. Remember that sale you made that one time where you were just so excited you could jump for joy? Sales, and by extension, serving others, is a very rewarding career. When the prospect agrees that what you have to offer, for the price you are offering it, is in fact what they need, a huge rush of dopamine hits the brain—and you have a sale.

However, not all the fish we catch are great. Sometimes we realize the fish we caught aren't exactly what we expected, and they leave a funny taste in our mouth. David Moora, a tailor from Massachusetts, admits, "I'm a people pleaser—sometimes to the detriment of myself and the company. I bend over backwards to please someone, and sometimes I fall into the trap."

Ah, yes. I sympathize with Moora on this. This is the "demanding and cheap" client. This client is challenging and lives in the Hassle Zone of the Ideal Client Matrix we looked at earlier. Some clients want everything you have at the lowest possible price and complain about everything. I'm sure you have a client or two like this.

Other times, we catch a big fish. When I talked to Pat Tuure, founder of Out There Web Designs in Ohio, he said his favorite clients paid long-term retainers, came to him with questions, contacted him when they needed help, and never got upset. Sounds like a fantasy, but it's not. These clients fall perfectly into the nice and easy client definition and fit well into the Ideal Client Zone of the Ideal Client Matrix. This is what we are looking for.

Certainly, the excitement of gaining business and getting a check is quite a rush. Because that dopamine hits so strong, we find ourselves saying, "Yes! Yes! Yes!" to everyone who wants to hire us. Then we experience the pluses and minuses of taking on every client. They become those challenging lessons we chalk up to rookie mistakes, and then we vow to be more careful next time.

The struggles with our primal instinct are real and painful. The survival stage of any business is not for the faint of heart. The highs are high; the lows are low, and contentment comes and goes. To survive the first few years, we find ourselves running between opposite ends of the spectrum and everywhere in between saying, doing, thinking, and feeling things we never dreamed we would say, do, think, or feel. Owning a business can be fun and easy, yes. But it generally only comes when we work hard to ensure we know who we want to work with.

**As a reminder, in the Survival Stage, we...**

| SAY | DO | THINK | FEEL |
|---|---|---|---|
| • Yeah, baby new business!<br><br>• I need sales.<br><br>• Yes, yes, yes! To all clients.<br><br>• I need money. | • Work late nights and weekends.<br><br>• Take on more clients, any clients, any heartbeat.<br><br>• Struggle.<br><br>• Give up self-care family, friends, vacations, time off. | • Is this what owning a business it?<br><br>• Profits? How?<br><br>• How am I going to pay the bills?<br><br>• I'm desparate for money. | • Excited.<br><br>• Frustrated.<br><br>• Overwhelmed.<br><br>• Exhausted.<br><br>• Sad.<br><br>• Disappointed. |

At the point of exhaustion and frustration in the survival stage, we pause to ask ourselves, "Does it have to be this difficult? What's next?" We record our lessons learned in our head, or our journal, and vow to do better in the future, whether that be the next day, month, or year.

If you feel as though you are in the survival stage right now, here are four things you can do to move on to the next more quickly.

1. **Start the process of finding and focusing on a target market.**

   If you don't already have a target market identified, use the Customer Profile Worksheet created by Ronii Bartles and located in the appendix to help you understand what markets your current clients fall into and if you might like working with these clients and their industry. If you aren't sure what industry to target after doing this worksheet and exercise, simply focus on finding the common threads. That will lead you to an industry that is ideal for you.

2. **Increase your price by 30 percent.**

   This is very general and may not work for everyone, but depending on what you are currently charging, you likely have room to increase the price of many of your services by at least an additional 30 percent. I know this from working with small business owners who happen to be in this stage, and they almost all undercharge. They set their price low to attract customers, but it works against them. Increase your pricing across the board.

3. **Set boundaries.**

   Stop working nights and weekends. If you need to gradually do this, that is fine, but please don't take longer than thirty days to move away from nights and weekends. If you can do it immediately, do so. This will allow you (force you, actually) to remain focused during your workday, increasing your productivity.

4. **Be productive.**

   Your time is the most precious commodity you have. Use it wisely. Do the tasks that only *you* can do—outsource the rest. Find ways to be more efficient and productive in your work day.

# CHAPTER 8

# SECURITY STAGE

Quick Assessment—How do I know if I'm in the Security Stage?

**Do you say, do, think, or feel any of the following?**

| SAY | DO | THINK | FEEL |
|---|---|---|---|
| • I'm almost there!<br><br>• You want me to do what? Okay.<br><br>• What value do I bring? | • Working late nights and weekends.<br><br>• Strive for consistency.<br><br>• Set goals. | • I need a few more clients.<br><br>• I don't like saying no.<br><br>• Challenging clients are worth the extra money.<br><br>• What vacation? | • A little better.<br><br>• A bit more stable.<br><br>• I can't say no to prospects, but wish I could. |

## STAGE SUMMARY

If you can relate to any of these things, then you are likely in the security stage. Generally speaking, many owners find themselves in the security stage at around twelve to twenty-four months in business. It depends, of course, on the business itself, its growth, and how quickly they can emerge from the survival stage. The things we say, do, think, and feel when we are just starting to get our feet under us bring us to this stage.

As you look over the chart, if you do not identify with any of the items, then it's probably okay if you want to jump ahead to the next stage. However, don't blame me if you miss a good story about how I created more consistent cash flow in my business.

---

Failing in the first year in business is the first statistic we have to overcome. Once we've knocked out that goal, we need to find a sense of security. However, surviving that first year doesn't mean taking risks will be comfortable. In fact, many small business owners are not at all comfortable with taking risks. Just because we took a risk in starting our own business does not mean we will always take risks, or take the right risks at the right time.

## OUR NEXT PRIORITY BECOMES SECURITY

Making safe decisions that offer a sense of security often becomes our priority. With security comes more certainty and less fear. As we become more comfortable with and confident in our ability to manage a business, security becomes the byproduct. With security and confidence, we often find more clients. However, we often think we need as many clients as we can get. The reality is most small businesses don't need thousands or even hundreds of clients. A nice, steady, manageable stream of well-suited, well-paying clients could provide consistent cash flow and more than enough revenue to create a stable and effective business.

In the survival and security stages, the objective is to survive, be consistent, and grow into a truly sustainable business with income that is predictable. When you have *predictable* revenue, you'll find a sweet spot, and you'll gain more confidence in your decisions, including in identifying best-fit clients.

In the early stages of our business, we are often burning the candle at both ends. During this time, we periodically find opportunities for improvements that greatly benefit all areas of our business. We also identify the parts of our business that are the well-oiled machine we dreamed of. That's when we start thinking about the services we offer, the good clients, and how to increase our revenue faster. With increased confidence, we feel excited once again, like when we first opened our doors. Our confidence starts to show more because we have learned so much. Then, we can start to make changes to achieve the next set of goals we set for ourselves.

## BUSINESSES CHANGE

Have you met a business owner who seems to change their business every time you see or talk to them? Maybe their company started off as a marketing agency, then it was social media management, and now it's graphic design. What? How does that happen?

Some people will look at this business owner as if they aren't really sure what they are doing and/or have limited business skills. Some people look at this as though these business owners are just out to make a sale. While it's true that some people fall into this category, most of them are not focused on the money at all. In fact, they are evolving as business owners. They are learning what markets are ideal for them and what services their clients need the most.

As a result of our own evolution, our businesses change, and we start to move toward the work that brings us more joy.

In this case, I believe this business owner is likely testing the market (something we should all do throughout the entire life of our business). From there, they can determine where the greatest value for their business lies. The ultimate goal here is to find the right market, service, and pricing so the business can evolve into a long-term, profitable business. From time to time, it's important to pause, assess, and remain focused on the end goal: More money, more time, and more freedom.

## FOLLOW YOUR TALENT

One of the most exciting things we get to do when we start a business is define our list of services. "This is what I do well, and this is how I can help others." Often, the list changes over the course of the business. It could change based on:

- What you like most
- Which clients you like most
- Market and industry trends

- Pricing
- External economic factors
- A pandemic
- Natural disasters
- All kinds of other reasons

The thing to remember is to be flexible enough to change when needed, and strong enough to know your own talents and what *you* like to do. Remember, just because you *can* do something doesn't mean you *have* to or *should* do something.

Katharine Giovanni, a business coach from North Carolina, advises her clients, "The direction people tell you to go is not often the direction you should take. Don't chase the money." Giovanni has a powerful point here. One reason we went into business for ourselves was because we wanted more money. However, chasing the money is a trap. Because everyone can see you doing it. Too often, business owners are given advice about focusing on sales and selling hard. Those are two different things, and they are often interpreted as *sell, sell, sell.*

Unfortunately, when we are in the Security Stage, we usually don't push back on prospects who ask us to lower our price. Instead, we take on these clients because we need the money to move out of the Security Stage. Melissa Noto, a graphic designer from Bolingbrook, Illinois, told me, "In the beginning, I would just say I'm extremely flexible. Because I didn't want to lose them. And I didn't have time to go out and find clients."

Noto brings up a key point. Finding clients takes time, and because we don't know when or where the next client is coming from, we often take the client who is in front of us, rather than risk losing them and not having another client come along. All too often, however, the client isn't a good fit for a number of reasons and ends up staying with us too long, taking up too much of our time, or not paying us enough money. It's a drain for sure. I bet you've had a few clients you thought weren't worth the hassle. Perhaps they even negotiated and ended up paying less than your standard rate, yet expected the same or even better service than other clients.

I correlate it to this. I'm a pizza guy. If you know me, you know I love a good pie. It's as if the prospects are looking to buy the whole pizza, but they only want to pay for a single slice. Don't even bother with these folks; it's a losing proposition. They'll waste a ton of your time. You'll make less money, and they will slow you down in your goal of achieving security.

When you lower your price to gain more clients, it slows upward movement on the Client Acquisition Hierarchy of Needs, limiting your ability to move to the next stage, and in some cases, moves you backward. Security is about finding and maintaining predictable revenue so you can become more selective about which clients you work with. However, if you constantly take on clients who cost you money, you are likely to become much more desperate and take on more of the same clients, keeping you from reaching the next stage of the hierarchy.

One of the best things you can do to gain stability and exit the Security Stage *like a boss* is to find great clients who provide that security blanket you need. Andrea Goodman, a business consultant from Massachusetts, had a great suggestion. She said, "Look for clients like you. My best clients are those who have high ethical standards and are collaborative and respectful. I appreciate those attributes because it's how I operate my business. So that's who I look for."

I love this idea because I'm all about relationships in business. Relationships are one of the key ways I find joy in business. I love surrounding myself with awesome people. Even if some of these folks aren't buying or paying for the highest level of service I offer, I still enjoy being around them, and I find great joy in working with them. Ultimately, that makes me a happier person.

Remember, even though clients don't always refer, when they do, they often refer people like themselves.

Another great message is embedded in what Katharine Giovanni said: "Other people rarely know what's best for you. That's for you to decide. Follow your inborn talents." When you follow your inborn talents, you'll be sure to advance quickly beyond security and toward joy.

With great effort and sound business decisions, you'll quickly emerge from the Security Stage while establishing a true base of clients and predictable revenue. Once you start making decisions about your ideal client, you will feel less pressure to take on difficult clients.

## CREATING STEADY INCOME

Pricing, services, and multiple revenue streams tend to be the golden tickets for a steady income. While this book is not about pricing strategies, service offerings, or multiple revenue streams, I did want to give you a few ideas and pointers to get you started in the right direction. Not all of these will work in your business; however, I encourage you to get creative and find ways to modify them to fit. Lack of steady income is the bane of business owners' existence. Without it, we risk failure.

Subscription services are all the rage right now because they offer guaranteed monthly or annual income. Subscriptions save time from a management perspective. By charging people monthly, you create your own version of a gym membership, resulting in great income.

Consider billing customers on their signup date instead of the first of the month. Many services bill on the first of the month. I recommend staggered billing for a couple of reasons. First, it can stabilize your monthly income and spread-out charges and deposits throughout the month so you don't have crazy spikes. Second, when the first of the month comes and your bill is added to ten others, your clients might start rethinking the cost of working with you. If you bill on their renewal date, they are less likely to be concerned about the bill and think about cancelling. Additionally, subscription services (monthly billing) allow you to sell your product or service at the annual price you want divided by twelve more easily digested monthly payments. Consider breaking up bigger invoices into smaller monthly payments. You're more likely to get people to sign up.

During the economic downturn of 2008, my digital agency was six years old, three years part-time and three years full-time. When the economy crashed, we scrambled to sell $6,000 websites. Clients were much harder to come by. Cash was tight for everyone. We especially struggled when the quote exceeded $10,000. But sometime in 2019, we had an epiphany. We could let customers make payments. So, we immediately rolled out six-month, interest-free financing. Basically, we took the quote price and divided it by six. The customer, if they agreed to sign with us, would then make six equal payments over the next six months. That changed the game for us. We had very little pushback. That payment arrangement did more than just help get us customers. It leveled out our cash flow and helped our clients with their cash flow. This was a true win-win situation. We were still using those payment terms the day I sold the agency.

Start looking for additional revenue streams, but keep them close to what you are already doing. At the agency, we offered multiple services, all of which were website-related, from hosting to management. At one point, we offered website backup and email hosting services. Countless options for expansion are built into your business; you just need to look at what you offer and what your clients need. Look at your competitors' websites for services you are not offering and maybe even have not thought of. The risk with adding services is drifting out of your lane. Too often, I see small business owners talking about an offering that has nothing to do with their current business. If you want to diversify your income and have multiple income streams, you need to ensure you clearly understand what you offer and how it fits in with your core business.

As we exit the Security Stage and graduate from the two core needs stages, Survival and Security, we're ready for the next challenge: the Discovery Stage. That's when everything really starts to shift.

**As a reminder, in the Security Stage, we...**

| SAY | DO | THINK | FEEL |
|---|---|---|---|
| • I'm almost there!<br><br>• You want me to do what? Okay.<br><br>• What value do I bring? | • Working late nights and weekends.<br><br>• Strive for consistency.<br><br>• Set goals. | • I need a few more clients.<br><br>• I don't like saying no.<br><br>• Challenging clients are worth the extra money.<br><br>• What vacation? | • A little better.<br><br>• A bit more stable.<br><br>• I can't say no to prospects, but wish I could. |

If you feel as though you are in the Security Stage right now, here are four things you can do to accelerate your progression to the next stage.

1. **Find or create an accountability group.**

   Working with colleagues you trust, meet at regular intervals and share what you're working on and your wins. Use the accountability group to get feedback and brainstorm growth ideas for your business.

2. **Create a recurring revenue service.**

   Do you currently have an offering that can be turned into a monthly subscription service? Many clients I work with have something, but they just haven't thought of it as a recurring service, billed monthly throughout the year.

3. **Increase recurring fees.**

   If you already have a recurring service offering, review your current fees and find a way to increase them. Increase them at least 10 percent, but ideally, go for a 20 percent increase.

4. **Set a sales goal.**

   Sales activities are a top priority as you push toward security. Your emphasis should be on sales activities, not so much closing sales. Sales activities are tasks you do that move you closer to a sale. If you produce revenue daily, you'll reach your sales goals, provided they are reasonable.

# CHAPTER 9

# DISCOVERY STAGE

Quick Assessment—How do you know if you're in the Discovery Stage?

**Do you say, do, think, or feel any of the following?**

| SAY | DO | THINK | FEEL |
|-----|-----|-------|------|
| • I can finally go on a vacation!<br><br>• I've made it this far!<br><br>• Let's do this!<br><br>• I'm doing something right! | • Ignite booster; let's grow!<br><br>• Automatic processes.<br><br>• Take risks; turn prospects away; off-load clients.<br><br>• Go after bigger clients with bigger budgets<br><br>• Charge what I'm worth. | • I'm earning a living!<br><br>• Am I respected? Am I valued?<br><br>• My business is surviving.<br><br>• What do I really want?<br><br>• If you value me, you'll pay the fees. | • Safe.<br><br>• Excited.<br><br>• Energized<br><br>• Hopeful. |

## STAGE SUMMARY

If you can identify with any of these items, you are likely in the Discovery Stage. Generally speaking, after two years, many business owners find themselves in this stage. Sometimes this stage lasts twelve months, and sometimes it lasts twelve years (although I certainly hope it doesn't take that long for you).

The things we say, do, think, and feel in the Discovery Stage lead us to change what we do. The Discovery Stage is all about discovering who we are as a person, what our business is, and what we are willing to accept.

As you look over the chart, if you do not identify with any of the items, it's probably okay to jump ahead to the next stage. However, don't blame me if you miss the explanation of my process for continuous action and improvement.

---

#High5—We made it! We've achieved stability in our business. Now what?

In the Discovery Stage, we shift from survival and the constant need for security to drastically embracing positive thoughts. The business is wrapped in a security blanket, having been carefully woven in the last stage, and now we are ready for breakthroughs and growth. As we enter the Discovery Stage, we simultaneously enter the Growth Band of the Business Owners' Hierarchy of Needs. We can consider these the coming of age years, like our business is a teenager, except with fewer pimples and definitely a lot less drama.

# CLIENT ACQUISITION
# HIERARCHY OF NEEDS

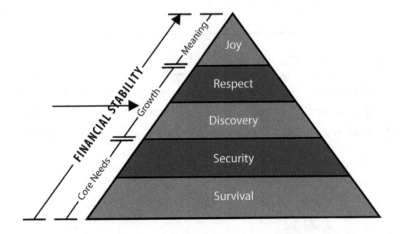

As we continue to grow as business owners, we start to look inward and discover more of what we want from our business and from ourselves. Inward reflection drives growth both personally and professionally. The Discovery Stage, regardless of how long it takes, is when we take a step back, review where we've come from, and take a deep dive into ourselves to decide what we want our business to look like moving forward. If we discover who we have become since we started our business, it can drive us to a new focus or goal. Additionally, we examine ourselves to find what we no longer enjoy and what no longer serves us. Eliminating roadblocks prepares us to attract the right clients, and ultimately, *joy*.

This stage is when we shed what doesn't suit us so we can reach our ultimate goal: building a business with clients who bring us *joy*.

As I mentioned previously, I was fortunate enough to interview more than fifty small business owners for this book. During that process, I talked with Gary Wilbers, a business coach and consultant from Jefferson City, Missouri. Wilbers said he deeply desires mutually beneficial relationships with his clients. "I don't have the energy to work with people who wear me out. I want to work with people who energize me." This is a powerful discovery, and it's exactly what happens in this stage.

## PATIENCE IS KEY

When you take that inward look, you may discover some things immediately, while discovering others may take a bit longer. Sometimes personal reflection and growth take time. Personally, I find that looking inward by myself takes far more time than when I work with clients to do the exact same thing. Perhaps it's because I work better in collaboration with others. My creative ideas often stem from seeds planted by others in conversation. In fact, my collaborative approach produces far better results in much less time than if I spend time alone thinking about where I want to improve. From time to time, things do come to me. But often, they come during very busy times during my workday and are triggered by other things I'm doing. I find when I sit alone and think, looking for a solution to a problem, I rarely find it, and if I do, it's a struggle. I can get frustrated just sitting and thinking. In talking with others, I often find that something that took them thirty minutes to discover took me three hours.

You may find that your process and results are similar, but make no mistake, regardless of how you get there, you need to think inwardly during the Discovery Stage so you can, in fact, discover what it is you want and how it fits into your business.

Something interesting emerged during the interviews I conducted with business owners. I found many became frustrated while developing the core needs (Survival and Security). But during the Discovery Stage, they shifted, creating systems and processes that ensured they made sound business decisions.

Ultimately, the time comes, or the stage, you could say, when we've had enough—enough bad clients, enough bad systems, enough bad days—and we create change. Larry Winget, also known as The Pitbull of Personal Development®, said, "People only change when the pain of not changing is so great there is no other choice."

Whether it's the process of selecting clients or the process of getting work done, we need to have some sort of system that works for us. John Ela, a CEO consultant from New Hampshire, said he created a process that made his life much easier and helped him develop standard requirements for accepting clients. "Every customer looks good when you see them as revenue and not a relationship," Ela said. To avoid a negative experience with future clients, he evaluates them after the first conversation. While the encounter is still fresh in his mind, he lists the pros and cons from what he learned, and he notes the worst thing that could happen with the client. Ever since, he has only worked with his ideal client. And those clients bring him joy.

Looking back at previous clients, Ela identified what mattered to him most and where he could find more joy in his business. Ela has followed this process for several years now, and it is still working great to this day.

Do you have a similar process for selecting your ideal clients? Have you looked at your current systems and processes to identify what can be improved to ensure you will work with clients more likely to bring *joy*?

In my twenty-plus-year career, I have tried so many things. I'm happy to be able to use just 20 percent of what I tried. I see that as a success. I continue to try new ways of doing things. It's an iterative process. In fact, it's one I jokingly refer to as "shitterating." Shitterating is the process of improving what you currently have by trying and testing new things, and keeping only what works from those new tests, while throwing out what doesn't work. The goal for me is to improve my systems and process by just one percent each time I "shitterate." I let go of what is not working in that process, and I keep what works. Then I move on to the next iteration. I just keep trying and moving things forward. I'm constantly looking for micro improvements in my business.

Experiencing *joy* in business is like a blast of fresh air. It makes a lot of the struggles worth it and gives us great hope for our business' future success.

**In the Discovery Stage, we...**

| SAY | DO | THINK | FEEL |
|---|---|---|---|
| • I can finally go on a vacation!<br><br>• I've made it this far!<br><br>• Let's do this!<br><br>• I'm doing something right! | • Ignite booster; let's grow!<br><br>• Automatic processes.<br><br>• Take risks; turn prospects away; off-load clients.<br><br>• Go after bigger clients with bigger budgets<br><br>• Charge what I'm worth. | • I'm earning a living!<br><br>• Am I respected? Am I valued?<br><br>• My business is surviving.<br><br>• What do I really want?<br><br>• If you value me, you'll pay the fees. | • Safe.<br><br>• Excited.<br><br>• Energized<br><br>• Hopeful. |

If you feel as though you are in the Discovery Stage right now, here are four things you can do to accelerate your progress to the next stage.

1. **Place a small journal on your desk and write your thoughts.**
   One of the biggest challenges is really discovering how you feel about something. By keeping a small journal on your desk, you

can quickly jot down a note about something that made you feel a certain way.

2. **Schedule a vacation.**

   Right now, talk about and schedule a vacation, even if it's just a short one. Just be sure to make it longer than what you have done in the past two years or so. That likely means it's a bit longer than a long weekend.

3. **Take time for lunch.**

   Taking an actual lunch break might sound like a lame idea; however, from experience, I know that when you change your physical environment, your mind can focus on other things. If you eat your lunch at your desk, you'll continue to work. If you take it away, or even out of the office, you'll get a breath of fresh air and maybe some new ideas or direction. If you really want to increase your awareness, have lunch with another human being (same one or different one) every day. This interaction will allow you to be more present in your lunch than being present in your work.

4. **Create a positive environment.**

   Find ways to improve your workspace by including more positive messaging. Consider printing positive quotes and hanging them on your wall, or writing Post-it notes with positive messages and putting them on your monitor. Surround yourself with positivity and your outlook about your work and your business will drastically improve over the next month!

# CHAPTER 10

# RESPECT STAGE

Quick Assessment—How do you know if you're in the Respect Stage?

**Do you say, do, think, or feel any of the following?**

| SAY | DO | THINK | FEEL |
|---|---|---|---|
| • I make good money. <br><br> • Money isn't everything. | • Take a vacation. <br><br> • Take a day off. | • I've earned this! <br><br> • I've gained some status. <br><br> • Relationships are growing. <br><br> • I want more peace. | • Accomplished. <br><br> • Energized. <br><br> • Productive. |

## STAGE SUMMARY

If any of this sounds like you, then you are likely in the Respect Stage. I've not really seen a time frame for the Respect Stage. In general, this stage creeps up on business owners and is often brewing in the background.

The things we say, do, think, and feel in the Respect Stage lead us to believe more strongly in ourselves, and that often results in others respecting us as well.

The Respect Stage is all about respecting ourselves, respecting our business, and having others respect us and our business.

As you look over the chart, if you do not identify with any of these things, then it's probably okay if you jump ahead to the next stage. However, don't blame me if you miss a good story about some awards.

---

R-E-S-P-E-C-T. Respect! This word can be a verb or a noun. In all my interviews with service-based business owners, I found respect to be one of the most common necessities business owners require from their clients and other professionals.

Through hard work, you have survived the first few years, built a secure foundation, and discovered what you wanted for you and your business. The years of constantly working through late nights and weekends, growing the business, and building relationships are finally paying off.

Gaining status and respect from your clients, colleagues, community, and industry is a definite feather in your cap. That feather, regardless of how you interpret it, provides confidence! It's this feather of respect that you've gained that propels you forward through the second stage of the growth band to reach higher heights.

We are never without challenge or conflict. At this point in our business, we need to (actually we must) strengthen our stance and approach to handle various situations. We must remember, there is no such thing as "autopilot" in business. Boy, wouldn't that be nice?

When I owned my agency, I often wondered if I was making an impact. From time to time, I would hear from clients who were happy with our services. That felt good, but I was still in that mode where I felt like I had to justify so much. That was until I got an email I will never forget in June of 2011. It arrived in the afternoon with the subject line "Congratulations!" It was a notification stating I had been selected as a "Forty Under Forty" winner for the *Worcester Business Journal*.

I was stunned! Maegen McCaffrey, a business colleague, had nominated me. That year and the years before, I had been involved with quite a few organizations, including several local chambers of commerce. In fact, I think I was a member of four different chambers at that time. Maegen was the executive director of one of the chambers, and the chamber was also a client. Because I was so involved with the chamber, and there was a great deal of interaction, Maegen knew me well. She felt it was appropriate to nominate me for this prestigious award. As they say, just to be nominated was an honor. I never actually thought I would win. But I did, and that's where respect entered the mix for me. I finally felt the work I had been doing for so many years, both with my clients and the business community, was paying off.

Being nominated for this award meant that people in the business community, like Maegen, *respected* what I brought to the table. The fact that I won the award also meant that those involved in the judging felt similar sentiments. This award raised my profile. However, more importantly, it increased my own self-respect, which also increased my confidence as a business owner.

Then. It. Happened. Again.

The next award came from another chamber, which awarded me the Chamber Small Business Owner of the Year award. Say what? In 2015, I was selected as the Chamber Small Business Owner of the Year by my local chamber of commerce. Maegen was not part of this chamber. This was a completely different organization. This was the second major award I had received in business, and I was blindsided by it. I did not know I was nominated, and I never knew I was being considered. It came as a complete surprise. This award was special because it showed me I was respected in my community, one in which I did *not* grow up. I'm sure you may know how difficult it is sometimes to fit into a new place that has many existing relationships that date back decades to when the current business owners were in high school, and even grade school together. So, yes, *respect* from clients, colleagues, and the community are feathers in the cap that many of us strive for. With hard work and tenacity, and by nurturing relationships over time, we gain respect.

## CONFIDENCE MATTERS

With each win, we build on something we have already achieved. Our foundation becomes even stronger. With a stronger foundation, we find the confidence needed to believe in ourselves. Layer upon layer, we create the internal fortitude we use to conquer the challenges we face, including making difficult decisions. Simply put, confidence matters, and it's a contributing factor in reaching *joy*. We'll dig much deeper into this in Part II, the Value Phase, but for now, just know that your confidence contributes greatly to your success—confidence, not cockiness. Note the difference.

**In the Respect Stage, we...**

| SAY | DO | THINK | FEEL |
|---|---|---|---|
| • I make good money.<br><br>• Money isn't everything. | • Take a vacation.<br><br>• Take a day off. | • I've earned this!<br><br>• I've gained some status.<br><br>• Relationships are growing.<br><br>• I want more peace. | • Accomplished.<br><br>• Energized.<br><br>• Productive. |

You've worked hard to achieve your level of success and respect from others. Now, you can breathe a bit, take a day off here and there, and even go on a vacation. While you have the money, you don't yet quite have the extra time and flexibility you may desire, but you are inching toward that ultimate goal. And yet, there is still more, something intangible you can't quite name, but you know you need it. You know you want respect, and it will make all the difference.

If you feel as though you are in the Respect Stage right now, here are four things you can do to accelerate your progression from this stage to the next.

1.  **Start by respecting yourself.**
    Respect comes with the understanding of what that really is.
    If we respect ourselves, our time, our business, and our skills,
    then we can expect respect from others.

2.  **Have a conversation with a colleague.**
    One place to start understanding if you have gained the respect
    of others is to have a conversation with a colleague. I recom-
    mend starting the conversation off with why you respect them.
    Then continue the conversation so you can get an understand-
    ing of why they respect you.

3.  **Pick one person you respect and talk to them.**
    When you surround yourself with others, you increasingly
    take on their attributes. This was summarized by Jim Rohn
    when he said, "You are the average of the five people you spend
    the most time with." By selecting people you respect to talk to
    and surround yourself with, you'll add people to your life who
    respect you. Don't just talk to them once, though; you need to
    build a relationship.

4.  **Be on time.**
    If you tend to show up right on time, or even "socially late," fix
    that. Start showing up early. Publicly, you may be getting a pass
    on being tardy, but privately, it is hurting your brand. Those
    who show up a little early and are ready to go on time often feel
    those who are late don't respect their time. Take action today
    to fix the tardiness and show up early to virtual and in-person
    meetings and events.

# CHAPTER 11

# JOY STAGE

Quick Assessment—How do you know if you're in the Joy Stage?

**Do you say, do, think, or feel any of the following?**

| SAY | DO | THINK | FEEL |
|---|---|---|---|
| • I get *joy* from others.<br><br>• I bring *joy* to others. | • More *joy* = more freedon,<br><br>• Time with family.<br><br>• Time for self-care. | • I'm much happier all around<br><br>• Positive thoughts about my next vacation?<br><br>• I love my clients. | • *Joy.*<br><br>• Happiness.<br><br>• Successful. |

## STAGE SUMMARY

If you identify with any of these things, then you are likely in the Joy Stage.

These are the things we say, do, think, and feel when we are in the Joy Stage that lead us into a much more fruitful and emotionally happy business.

The Joy Stage is all about reaching a level in our business that brings us joy, and ultimately, more money, more time, and more freedom.

As you look over the chart, if the items don't resonate for you, it's okay to drop back to a previous stage where you will find some tactics to get you back up to Joy.

---

Welcome to the final stage of The Client Acquisition Hierarchy of Needs! By this time in your business, you recognize your own achievements. You may be surprised by the decisions, directions, struggles, and people you've encountered along the way, or you might feel like you knew they were there all along. Perhaps you are just getting started in business and looking for signs (red flags) of things to avoid so you will have a more sustainable business much quicker.

This final stage, *Joy*, becomes an iterative stage whereby we keep working on what joy means to us, defining that joy, and working to remove whatever is not joyful and include more of what is. It's similar to a snowball. As you start the snowball, it is small, not heavy, and doesn't have much momentum, but as you keep rolling it and adding more snow, it gains mass, weight, and speed. Eventually, the snowball rolls all the way down the hill without any assistance. Your business is similar in that if you continue to make decisions focused on achieving joy, the business will run itself without much involvement from you in the future. That will surely give you more money, more time, and more freedom.

Each challenge, struggle, decision, direction, and person who comes along in your journey is there for a reason. Through each of them, you have matured, learned, overcome, succeeded, and filled your need to understand how important client discernment, selection, and acquisition is to your business' success. It's a long journey, but a worthwhile one.

Embracing these specific needs further allows you to enjoy the fruits of your labor: more money, more time, and more freedom. In addition, when you are valued and respected by others, it increases your self-respect, self-esteem, and confidence. Furthermore, when you build a business based on relationships and clients you want to work with, you build a business that brings you *joy*.

*"There is no greater feeling than experiencing joy in business!*

*It drives every aspect of my business life!"*

— Matt Ward

In the Joy Stage, we...

| SAY | DO | THINK | FEEL |
|---|---|---|---|
| • I get *joy* from others. <br><br> • I bring *joy* to others. | • More *joy* = more freedon, <br><br> • Time with family. <br><br> • Time for self-care. | • I'm much happier all around <br><br> • Positive thoughts about my next vacation? <br><br> • I love my clients. | • *Joy.* <br><br> • Happiness. <br><br> • Successful. |

Now that you understand the needs defined by the Client Acquisition Hierarchy of Needs, you are ready to discover your Value in Phase 2 of *The High Five Effect*.

# CLIENT ACQUISITION
# HIERARCHY OF NEEDS

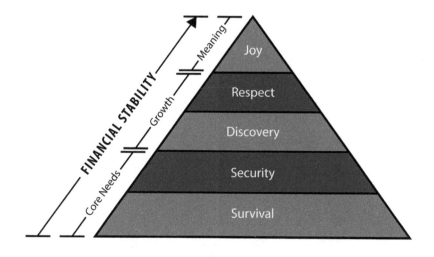

ARE YOU READY TO VALUE YOURSELF?

LET'S GO!

# PHASE II

# CHAPTER 12

# VALUE YOURSELF

"My momma always said, 'Life is like a box of chocolates, you never know what you're gonna get.'" Forrest Gump's momma in the movie *Forrest Gump* was certainly correct; we never do know what we are gonna get in life or in business. However, as business owners, it's our job and responsibility to build profitable businesses.

Let's examine a box of chocolates. A box of chocolates offers many varieties. How do you go about choosing which chocolates to eat first? Do you eat your favorites first or save the best for last? If you are like me, you might avoid the dark chocolates and go straight for the milk chocolate covered toffee, or how about that chocolate covered dipped cherry? Now...I'm hungry.

I very much value the experience of receiving a box of chocolates. Such a gift is always a delightful surprise, especially when the packaging is attractive with special paper or ribbons. Follow along in this experience with me. The box is in your hands. Untie the bow. Unwrap the paper. Lift off the lid. All of sudden, your senses are filled with the delicious aroma of the chocolate. Your eyes feast on the beautifully designed chocolate candies, each one containing a different surprise filling. Your heart might skip a beat in awe of the beauty. Your mouth waters with anticipation of the flavors. Your mind screams, "Which one?" And you hear your gut say, "Don't let anyone take your favorites!" Our brain immediately scrambles, "Which is your first, second, third choice? Make sure to leave some chocolate for others. Share with them. But take your favorites first."

Yes, I value each phase of the experience that a box of chocolate offers: receiving the gift, feeling surprise and gratitude, activating each of the six senses (the sixth is gut), choosing which beautiful piece to eat, and gracefully placing the scrumptious nugget in my mouth. I must say, it brings me great *joy*!

Valuing the experience of receiving chocolates can definitely offer chocolate lovers joy. Valuing ourselves is a critical part of the experience we offer ourselves and others when we own a business. If we don't value ourselves, it's actually a disservice to our business, clients, colleagues, community, industry, profits, family, and especially ourselves. Every so often, throughout a business' lifespan, it's necessary for owners to examine all areas of the business. We, the owners, need to look for opportunities for improvements and change.

We are all a work in progress. Whether business or personal, the way we feel about ourselves at various times changes. With all the variables of owning a business, sometimes we are so busy building, perfecting, or dealing with issues that we lose sight of the way we act on any given day when we interact with our clients, staff, vendors, and even families. When was the last time you performed an internal check of yourself and viewed yourself from your clients' perspective? How do you look to the world?

- Are you a confident business owner who knows their stuff?
- How important and relevant is your education, experience, and expertise?
- Do you have self-worth and self-respect?
- What are your strengths, weaknesses, and natural talents?
- In your business, do you perceive your products or services as necessary and helpful to your customers and clients?

When you read through the list above, do you feel as though you are rocking it? Or do you feel like you have areas you need to work on? Or perhaps, you feel you don't, can't, or won't live up to such expectations.

When we start looking at the aspects by which we value ourselves, there are many—really endless—thoughts and feelings that course through our mind and body.

When you reviewed the list, were there any strong reactions? Were most of your reactions good, bad, or in between? Do you feel some of your reactions are true and some are simply not true?

It's not easy for us to value ourselves. On a given day or in a matter of minutes, we can swing from high to low. At times, we feel as if we are on top of the world. Other times, we feel like we are at the bottom of the trash barrel. Why? Where does that come from? We have so much history from how we were raised, our environment, family, friends, society, and ourselves. These are things that feed into the image and belief we have about ourselves. This, of course, fluctuates like the stock market.

Dan Candell is a board-certified hypnotist. I've known Candell for many years, and I interviewed him for this book because I really wanted to get his insight into value.

Candell told me, "We all need to embrace what I refer to as the Bounce-Back Effect. That is where we embrace our inner resiliency to bounce back from negative times. The reason we get into funks is because we measure ourselves up against not only other people but also our past successes and our past failures."

He went on to say, "That's why I have the tagline I do, Matt: Be well, do good, and be true to who you are. Being true to who you are increases the value you bring to the world."

I pondered that for a minute; then I asked, because I really wanted to dig a bit deeper into this, "How does the Bounce-Back Effect apply to valuing ourselves?"

Candell said, "We all have core values, principles we hold true. When we are in a funk, we ignore those values, and that is when we allow others to take advantage of us. Bouncing back effectively allows us to hold true to our values in a much greater way."

Value really isn't about money, even though sometimes it's talked about in that way within a business.

"You see, Matt," Candell went on, "when you ask me about value, it's interesting because to me value has nothing to do with money. In fact, value is being true to who you are. Value is about understanding the core principles you hold near and dear to you as an individual. When people are chasing money, then they're not really fulfilling their value. If you have a high sense of value for yourself, you'll demand more from others. That's the big key in business, that you have to be true to who you are so you get those clients you want and who will fuel your values even more."

Candell is spot on with this. Furthermore, the funk he talks about can just be a small mental block around the work we do. It can be the inner critic questioning the quality of our work or the lack of detail we recently put into a project. If we bounce back from those thoughts to more positive ones, we get back to our core values much quicker.

You may be saying, "Yeah, but how I feel about myself is internal; no one else knows how I really feel about myself." Wrong. Everyone can feel it, sense it, and see it as your self-identity. Just like in poker, there are tells. How you value yourself reverberates around you. It's in your handshake, the way you walk into a room, and the way your voice cracks.

Your self-respect and confidence clearly show during pricing discussions. Yes, they do. Let's say you are negotiating a sale and you offer A, B, and C packages at three different prices, $1,000, $2,000, $3,000. Prospective client Chris really wants C for $3,000, but Chris can "really only afford" $1,000.

Right now, today, what would you do? If you are not secure in your own value, for any number of reasons, you are going to give Chris C for $1,000 (the highest value package for the lowest fee). The first reason is you need the money and some money is better than no money. The second reason is you don't value your worth enough to negotiate, and it might also be that you are unsure of yourself and your prices.

On the other hand, if you are confident in yourself and in the service you provide, you know that dropping your price, in this case drastically, lowers the value of your service. It also begins to erode your confidence about what you are worth. You know offering a deep discount is going to cost you money, and that matters to you.

The services you provide for package C may require three times as many hours as A, plus C requires a different level of output, which is going to set your client's business up well. The client gets the better end of the deal.

Instead, if Chris can only afford $1,000, then you need to sell Chris Package A. When someone wants what you offer for less than your fee, it's time to revisit what it is they can truly afford, but even more so, revisit the value you bring to the table and your overall worth. Look at the outcome your work produces for them, and when you come to that conclusion, increase the value you put on the work you do.

This scenario came up often at my digital marketing agency. For some reason, tech businesses seem to be obsessed with negotiating terms. Early on, I did it because I needed the money and was not confident enough in our services. Once I gained that confidence through the Survival and Security Stages, I did not do it again. I always responded to the prospect that we would need to remove items from the quote to keep the price within their budget. I would not deliver services at discounted prices anymore.

The way we think about ourselves is ever changing. This is why people spend thousands of dollars on self-improvement and self-help books. The good news is, we can change whatever it is we don't like. We are in control of our businesses, our thoughts, and our actions. We can reach the ultimate level, totally valuing ourselves in our business so we can achieve the dream of...

**MORE MONEY, MORE TIME, AND MORE FREEDOM**

## HOW DO WE VALUE OURSELVES?

Valuing ourselves brings us to the precipice of success in each area of business. Ironically, we don't consider valuing ourselves important enough because we think we can just go with the flow. I equate it to the importance of putting the oxygen mask on yourself first. We need to take care of ourselves first before we can take care of others.

Additionally, as a spinoff of the old love adage, ask yourself, "If you can't value yourself, why should clients value you and choose to work with you?" Fortunately, much like The Client Acquisition Hierarchy of Needs, we become more mature and comfortable with valuing ourselves as we build the business. We have room to learn, develop, and grow. Along the way, we'll also face hiccups and challenges, and sometimes, we will feel as though we flatline for a moment or two. With perseverance, support, and a can-do attitude, our hearts always beat again. It'll take a bit of work, but it's doable.

## VALUING YOURSELF—WHAT GETS IN THE WAY?

Sometimes, it feels as though a firehose has opened on us and is spewing nothing but negative messages. Other times, we feel high as a kite because everything seems to be going our way. How do we handle the extremes? Is there a way to prevent the negative and promote more positive messages? The good news is the answers are yes and yes. Yes, we can shut down the negative messages, and yes, we can promote more positive messages.

We often value ourselves on what we say and do and how we think and feel about ourselves, plus what others say, do, think, and feel about us. Whatever we feel and hear affects our confidence, self-worth, and self-respect. The highs are high, and the lows are low. The neutral times are really nice. Decisions we make and actions we take can either directly increase or decrease how we value ourselves. It's important to make clear, smart decisions for you—Y-O-U! After all, it's your business.

## MAKE SMART DECISIONS

"Don't forget your inborn talents!" stresses Katharine Giovanni, a business coach from North Carolina who works with executives. She often reminds clients that the way to find value in yourself is to use your own inborn talents to create products and services. "And don't follow the money!" she advises. "Following the money gets you in trouble because your business services or products tend to be focused on that and not what you naturally do well. It will eventually bore or frustrate you to the point of giving up and quitting. Then you no longer have a business." Instead, build a business around natural talents and the work you love to do. It will last longer, and I know you will definitely find *joy* in a business you love.

# CHAPTER 13

# NEGATIVE SELF-TALK AND THE CONFIDENCE SHREDDER

Pauline Robertson is a hair stylist, colorist, and the founder of Shear Transformation in Massachusetts. She told me, "Valuing yourself is about knowing what you do well. My goal is to do great hair and give great customer service." She further explains, "It takes experience to value yourself. In my earlier years, if a client didn't like their hair or complained, I started questioning myself: 'Should I be doing this? Do I suck at this? Should I quit?'"

Depending on how long we've been in business, chances are we've asked ourselves those same questions at least once. Those questions are negative self-talk and they shred confidence. They can destroy us and our business from the inside out, eating us alive. They do not belong in our head nor in our business. This situation only proves we really need to dig deep to define how we value ourselves. At some point, the questions will come back again, and if we know our own greatness and what we offer the world, we'll be able to squash the "Should I quit?" questions in no-time.

## IMPOSTER SYNDROME

Do you ever feel like a fraud in your business? Do you feel as if all the work you did to get where you are wasn't good enough and someone is going to find you out? Imposter syndrome is a real problem for a lot of people. It, too, can come and go or hang around and linger for life.

Arlin Cuncic explains imposter syndrome in his article for VeryWellMind.com as, "Internal experience of believing that you are not as competent as others perceive you to be."[2] Often, this idea is applied to our beliefs about our own intelligence or achievement. We can also encounter it in perfectionistic behavior or in social situations. Regardless of social status, work background, skills, or degree of expertise, we don't feel as if we belong and like we got where we are by luck.

William Salazar, a financial adviser from Boston, says, "It's so difficult to value ourselves because we're afraid. It's that imposter syndrome, the feeling that we are going to get 'found out.' We've all been brainwashed with this hustle mentality. So, if you are not hustling, you're not successful. So, we have these fake conversations with ourselves where we don't truly understand what we offer that is valuable to our customers."

If we walk around with the mindset that we don't belong or we don't have what it takes to run our business, how will our business succeed? Why will clients hire us? How will we be profitable? Undervaluing ourselves is not healthy, and it can damage our opportunities for success.

I have experienced imposter syndrome quite a bit in my business life. The chants internally of "I'm not good enough" never really manifested in a way that prevented me from taking action. In fact, I'm known as someone who takes "massive action." Here's the secret... Recognize the thoughts, but don't act on them; act in the exact opposite way of the thoughts. This is exactly how I deal with imposter syndrome. Recognizing the thoughts allows you to create a habit of seeing them and knowing what they look and sound like. This habit will ultimately result in a skill. Knowing when imposter syndrome is creeping in is a very valuable skill, one I wish we were born with, but alas, that is not the case. Once you recognize it and act in the opposite direction, you're moving away from the "concern" that the imposter

2 Imposter Syndrome, https://www.verywellmind.com/imposter-syndrome-and-social-anxiety-disorder-4156469

syndrome is focused on, and the end result is you will take more action in a more positive way.

## "COMPARANOIA®"

Compara...what? Comparanoia®. When you combine comparison and paranoia, you get the portmanteau, "Comparanoia®." Be sure to notice the registered trademark because it isn't my genius word. It belongs to its creator, author and speaker Davide Di Giorgio. I first learned the term from a colleague and friend, Larry Roberts, host and founder of *Readily Random Podcast*.

In a humorous, insightful, and very relevant blog post,[3] Roberts shared his reactions to attending Podfest, an annual conference for podcasters. Before we get to the real-life hilarity and fear he expressed in his article, let's first properly define the term, as offered in the blog with deference given to Di Giorgio.

Comparanoia®/kəm‚perə'noiə/Noun
The unresourceful beliefs, thoughts, feelings, behaviors, and/
or actions that come as the consequence of an incident or as
the result of not meeting or exceeding a goal, standard, bench-
mark, or expectation.

As Roberts said, it's easy for any of us to fall into the trap of comparing ourselves to others in our industries. He compares himself to podcaster Joe Rogan, whom he had delusions he could easily be like. Roberts expected that he would launch his podcast, and within a few days, he would watch the downloads spike up as millions of downloads broke the internet. In stark reality, the data showed ten to twenty downloads per episode. Sometimes, reality bites.

I feel his pain. I've attended conferences myself and seen large groups of people enjoying conversations while I sat alone across the hallway. At conferences and even networking events, I've found

---

3 Comparanoia® https://podcastbusinessjournal.
com/3-ways-to-overcome-post-podfest-comparanoia/

myself asking, "Who is that person everyone is talking to? What do I need to do to be them?"

If we do it for any length of time, and don't shut off our inner critic, we can feel Comparanoia® settling into our gut. Butterflies, pain, and nausea are a few symptoms we may feel when we have an inkling that something is wrong, or we don't feel "good enough."

"But good enough for whom?" we should ask ourselves. Even Oprah Winfrey started the movement, "I am enough." Why is it so hard to believe in ourselves? With imposter syndrome and now, Comparanoia®, how do we even stand a chance?

There is hope. It comes through valuing yourself. Developing a strong sense of self-worth, self-respect, and a high level of confidence is uber (yes, I said "uber") important, and it's the first step toward success. Because...I'll ask one more time...if we can't value ourselves, how will anyone else value us?

## WHY DOES RESPECT, SELF-WORTH, AND CONFIDENCE MATTER?

Here's something most people won't tell you—you need all three: self-respect, self-worth, and self-confidence to succeed at your greatest level. Why? Because consciously or unconsciously, how we feel about ourselves reflects what we believe about ourselves, and others can sense it. Others get a gut feeling, a sense of our confidence by the way we walk, talk, make decisions, and transact business.

*"But, as a business owner, I may not value myself in all areas: respect, worth, and confidence. Why should that matter? I have one of the three. Isn't that good enough?"*

No.

It's not good enough. If I'm a mother bear, and I have three cubs who need three meals a day to grow and get strong, can I decide that feeding them one meal a day is "good enough"? No. They wouldn't grow, they wouldn't become strong, and they would lag behind, unable to fulfill their life's purpose.

If you pick one of three or two of three, you will not grow in your mind, in your business, nor in your profits. You will not realize your full potential, nor fulfill your life's purpose.

Darlene Trainer is a business development employee in Massachusetts. She focuses on sales and client acquisition for her company. Remember our previous example of Packages A, B, and C? Darlene said, "If you have a difficult prospective client standing in front of you, you need to know that you value yourself; otherwise, you will cave at their every whim. It's a matter of self-respect and protecting yourself, your schedule, your efforts, your business, and your profits. If I don't value myself, I'm going to give them everything under the sun and *end up paying them* for *me to work for them.*"

Imagine that.

When you read that quote from Trainer, did you immediately recall that one client where you felt like you were paying them to do the work for them? Yeah...me too. We've all been there, usually in the early stages of our business.

When we value ourselves, we take the time to build the mission, create the vision, and communicate what we want to offer our clients, all based on how we perceive ourselves as a business owner.

I asked the small business owners who are members of my Facebook group, "How do you define 'Imposter Syndrome' as it relates to running your business?"

Nancy Pratt, former owner of Rock 'n Road Outfitters located in Auburn, Massachusetts, answered, "When other people think you're doing great and your business is thriving, but you still feel like you don't have any idea what the hell you're doing."

I think Pratt really sums this up well. I also believe she's right on point that when your business *is thriving*, you may still think you aren't doing great and don't know what you are doing. It's us, as business owners, telling ourselves a false narrative.

"I think imposter syndrome is a big piece of not valuing yourself enough," says Diane Reiner, a business owner in Wisconsin. "The ability to gauge our own self-esteem and self-worth has a direct effect on how we charge the appropriate fees to our customers. And most importantly, how we do not let them take advantage of us."

## HOW TO VALUE YOURSELF

The goal here is to shift to a *value mindset*. The next steps could be reading books, watching YouTube videos, hiring a coach, or seeing a therapist focused on professional development. It's not that difficult to improve. A serious and determined person will find the means to improve anything and everything they feel will help their overall goal and purpose.

## SHIFTING TO A *VALUE MINDSET*

I have found through the years that what I focus on is what I achieve. The more intentional my actions are toward something, the more likely I will achieve that goal. Furthermore, I'm likely to achieve it faster. My mindset is a big part of that. Action is driven by focus, and focus is driven by mindset. If we can shift our mindset to bring the focus into the fact that we have value, that focus alone will reframe our mind, refocus our efforts, and allow us to take a clearer, more definitive path of action.

After reading his blog post, I interviewed Roberts and found two of his perspectives to be relevant to my own mindset. "[A]s long as we focus on the wrong person, we are taking time away from our own creative process. Focus on what you have direct control over. Focus on what you can do to make your [business] the best possible business it can be."

*"We get so caught up in the comparisons and what we should be doing that we forget to celebrate our successes."*

— Larry Roberts, Host & Founder of *Readily Random Podcast*

Yes, it's time to value yourself. Here are a few ways you can start to improve your mindset about how you value yourself so you can start getting results.

- Stop comparing yourself to others. Start comparing yourself to your actions last week.

- Stop talking negatively to and about yourself. Start reciting a positive affirmation daily.
- Stop feeling as though you are an imposter. Start feeling empowered and that you belong.
- Get a book to learn how to address some of your insecurities. Start increasing self-improvement activities and stop avoiding corrective self-help action.
- Research affirmations and pick out those that relate to you. Start using them daily and place them around your office.
- Invest in Post-it notes with positive affirmations.
- Stop avoiding professional help and therapists. Start talking to a therapist and get some tools to combat negative self-talk and the inner critic.
- Stop avoiding help. Start working with a qualified coach to move from a B level player to an A level player.
- Stop commiserating over what's not working. Start celebrating your worth, respect, confidence, talents, strengths, weaknesses, education, experience, expertise, services, products, business, and successes.
- Stop the self-doubt. Start perceiving yourself as a confident business owner with major talent who has high levels of self-worth and self-respect and does not let anyone take advantage of them.

Now, the work is starting to get real. And it all starts with you!

## ARE YOU READY TO IDENTIFY?

## LET'S GO!

# PHASE III

# CHAPTER 14

# THE HIGH-FIVE EFFECT

"I feel the need...the need...for *speed*." High-five! Yes, the "high-five scene" in *Top Gun*, one of America's top fighter pilot movies, is a classic. It's ingrained into our memories as the perfect partnership in flight school and teamwork. It's the scene I want to see replayed again and again in my business with my clients. As I wrote in my previous book, clients hire people they know, like, trust, and *care* about. As a business owner, I want to work with clients, and other business partners, whom I can high-five and sit down together with for a beer. When I achieve such a strong bond with these people, I attribute it to what I call "The High-Five Effect." When I achieve this outcome, I know I have built a business with clients who bring me joy. You picked up this book because you want the same, so I'm going to share the formula that will help you achieve your goal to build a business with clients who bring *you* joy.

By design, I've created five phases for you to develop to achieve the High-Five Effect in your business. Building a business with clients who bring you joy is a continuously developing process. Before we reveal this new "identify phase," let's review the two phases covered earlier.

In the Introduction, you learned about "The Business Owner's Evolution of Joy," which depicted the five phases: Assess, Value, Identify, Strengthen, and Engage. We walked through how a business owner's journey evolves through these phases over time.

In **Assess**, we assessed our position in business using "The Client Acquisition Hierarchy of Needs," which laid out the basic needs of building a business with clients who bring you joy. Those stages included Survival, Security, Discovery, Respect, and Joy. As you graduate from each of these stages in your business, you start to say, do, think, and feel very differently from the previous stages. The hierarchy of needs is key for understanding how we progress in our business, as well as where we are currently.

In **Value**, we uncovered how to value ourselves so we can show up as confident business owners and leaders with high self-esteem and high self-respect. We learned how to keep the focus on a positive mindset so we can understand ourselves better, resulting in greater impact for us and for our business.

Here in **Identify**, we'll examine and identify clients who are not working well, as well as those who are working well and why it matters.

## TWO DIFFERENT TYPES OF CLIENT ENGAGEMENT

As previously stated, in business, we generally work with two types of clients: Transaction-Driven or Relationship-Driven. Because we meet and work with many different clients who have many different personality traits and business goals, this elixir of a cocktail can, at times, result in some rather dicey and explosive relationships. In fact, some clients may be more interested in transactional experiences and some may be more relationship-driven.

**Relationship-Driven** clients are people who thrive on relationships. They aren't focused entirely on the product or service you are delivering. In fact, they are often extremely interested in other things outside of the transaction. This type of client may engage in small talk and conversations that lead to topics that are personal in nature and not relative to the service you offer. Sometimes these clients fall into a subsection of your business where they hire you for long-term projects or retainer services. Through those services, in most cases, a strong, trusting, and long-standing relationship is developed. When the relationship is successful, it increases the longevity of your client relationship, their lifetime value, and your business' overall success. It drastically increases your ability to renew contracts and acquire referrals. However, the length of the service engagement is not the determining factor for a relationship-driven person. It is more about how they approach the relationship and whether they engage in conversation not relevant to the service being provided.

Relationship-driven clients and people are my jam! They drive me! I look forward to the conversations we have outside of the service I provide. Learning more about people and deepening our relationship is one major contributor to achieving *joy* in my business!

**Transaction-Driven** clients are those focused on the service being offered. They rarely engage in small talk, have little time for building any type of formal relationship, and are often very action or "transaction" focused. When this type of client approaches you for the service you offer, you give the client what they need, and the exchange is usually complete. They may come back later for more service. Sometimes, that is in the same year or two years later. Sometimes, it's even the next day or week, and when they do, they conduct the transaction in a similar fashion and move on. They often come across as people who don't have time to talk, and/or don't want to. And...that's okay!

## EITHER OR BOTH?

A relationship-driven person may first come across as transactional. That is because there may be limited interaction, and they may not have been able to build a relationship yet. That may come with time. Keep an eye out for this. Don't make the assumption that a person cannot go from transactional to relationship-driven, or vice versa. It can happen if the right ingredients are present. It's up to you to determine the type of client they are and work toward understanding the type of relationship they want moving forward.

As our business matures and we become more experienced as business owners, we also start to discover that our services work best for certain people, as well as our working styles, processes, and personalities.

Similar to our growth as business owners in "The Client Acquisition Hierarchy of Needs," our experiences with clients also develop over time. When we are new to the business, we take on clients for four main reasons:

1. We want to help. We believe and want our products and services to help people.
2. We are hungry for clients because we want more clients and clients drive growth.
3. We need the cash to grow the business. Saying yes brings in more cash.
4. We haven't yet become wise to the difference between "right-fit" and "wrong-fit" clients.

At the beginning, we are excited about business. This excitement shows through in our statements to others that we know our business will be a success because we are going to help people—all kinds of people! But then it happens. We take on *any* client out of direct necessity, simply because we need the cash to grow. See...to us...

**Clients = Cash!**

We need to build the business, and we need the cash to pay the bills. These are all reasons we might say "yes!" to anyone who expresses an interest in our services.

David Greenwood, author of *Overcoming Distractions,* founded his public relations business in 2005. Through it, he has learned the differences between clients he would put in the "Ideal Client Zone" and clients he would put in the "No-Go Zone."

When I interviewed David, he explained it like this:

> I think when you start a business, you take what you can get because you need the money. There is the beauty of building a business. Then, there is the building of a healthy business where you get to pick and choose your clients. There's always that fear that you're going to lose money. And sometimes we hang on to the clients or hang on to the business when we really don't want it because we have to keep going. You lose sleep at night because you have health problems, stress, and people you don't want to work with. That's a bad position to be in. When you have clients with really good relationships that respect your expertise and your opinion, you can have a meaningful dialogue about differences of opinion; that's the perfect relationship.

In the first year of owning a business, the love fest of working with people begins.

"I love what I do. I love my clients."

"It's so great working with this client! They really understand what we are doing for them, and they appreciate me and the results we provide."

"This client loves to collaborate on our project, and I really enjoy that approach. We work well together."

Then, after a while, maybe in your second or third year, you find yourself scratching your head wondering,

"How am I losing money?"

"What is up with this client?"

"Hold the phone! They aren't paying?"

The honeymoon of saying "yes" to everyone starts to wear off. "It's hard to please people sometimes," Jeff Gordon, founder of Ideal Video Strategies in Massachusetts, explains. "As a videographer, some of my clients don't understand how long the process takes to produce a video." For business owners, quality becomes a big concern. "A client of mine wanted me to clean up her audio recording that was done on her old phone. I explained it wasn't going to come out well, but I would do the best I could. It was not good, and she wasn't happy."

In speaking with Gordon, I found that in his previous conversations with the client, she would not acknowledge the quality of the audio in the old phone. She wouldn't even entertain the conversation. Eventually, when he delivered the product, she was dissatisfied and refused to pay him.

Now, that is not a good client. Not paying makes them not ideal; however, this was a client Gordon really knew he shouldn't have taken on. When she refused to talk about the quality of the original audio during the initial consultation, that was a red flag. She was destined to be a difficult client.

After running a digital marketing agency and participating in networking for so many years, I've met people who were struggling with all the same client issues. With all the discussions, I started connecting the dots and building profiles of similar client types. It was obvious that my original goals to achieve more money, more time, and more freedom, would take much longer than I ever expected. I continued to reflect on my processes, the services I offered, and the work I produced to figure out how I could improve my own business.

## FOUR TRUTHS OF CLIENT RELATIONS

It's safe to say we don't pick the wrong clients on purpose just to make our lives or their lives more difficult. It's the same process we follow when we learn we prefer milk chocolate over dark chocolate—trial and error. Rookie versus ace. It takes a long time to know the attributes we want to see in our "Ideal Client."

However, it's not as difficult as it sounds. The more we work with clients, the more we recognize four truths. Think about your current clients and see if any of these truths resonate for you.

1. Some clients are really great to work with and we can say they bring us joy.
2. Some clients are okay to work with and we don't care if they stay or go.
3. Some clients are sort of difficult to work with, and life may be better without them.
4. Some clients are really difficult to work with and we could say they bring us pain.

That we can clearly identify four types of clients tells me we need to be very aware of them while they are clients, but more so prior to bringing them on as a client. Now that you are aware of the four types, let me show you how they fit together and how to determine who is who. Let's check out the next chapter where I will show you the Ideal Client Matrix.

# CHAPTER 15

# THE IDEAL CLIENT MATRIX

When it comes to your clients, are you able to relate to the "Four Truths"? Let's dig further. I designed "The Ideal Client Matrix" with the following measurable components to help you identify where your clients fall when it comes to bringing *you* joy or causing you pain.

- The X-axis (horizontal line) measures the level of pain to joy you feel when working with your client.
- The Y-axis (vertical line) measures your engagement as transaction-driven or relationship-driven with your client.
- Within the four quadrants are two additional subsections, the interior and exterior. The interior segments are the Four Client Types.
  - Four Client Types
    - Adequate Clients
    - Challenging Clients
    - Risky Clients
    - Great Clients
- The exterior segments are what I call the "Client Zones":
  - Four Client Zones
    - The Blip Zone
    - The No Go Zone
    - The Challenging Zone
    - The Ideal Client Zone

# IDEAL CLIENT MATRIX

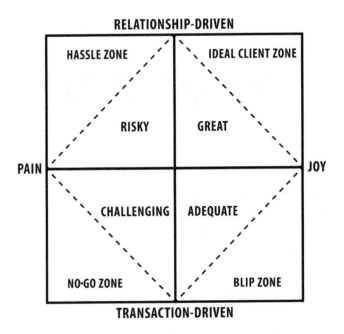

## THREE GOALS TO ACHIEVE USING THE IDEAL CLIENT MATRIX

As you look at the Ideal Client Matrix, you can assess where each of your clients falls in the quadrants. You are looking to achieve three goals when engaging in this process.

   1. **Clients Who Bring You** *Joy*—Identify which clients you like working with because of the following attributes:
      a. Relationship-driven
      b. Long-term
      c. Pay on time
      d. Respect your work
      e. Appreciate your offerings
      f. Bring joy in working together
      g. When you think of them, they make you smile

2. **Clients Who Cause You *Pain*—**Identify which clients would be best to let go of for the following reasons:
   a. More transactional
   b. Require more time than necessary
   c. Slow to pay or don't pay
   d. Complain
   e. Increase your level of frustration
   f. Bring you pain

3. **Move Clients from *Pain* to *Joy*—**It is possible, for various reasons, that you have clients who don't bring you complete joy, yet cause you very little pain. These clients may offer benefits if you keep them. Maybe the income is steady and losing the client would be worse than keeping them with a little pain. Ultimately, it comes down to your pain threshold and whether or not you want to put in the effort and attempt to move them closer to joy. It may be possible to move these clients from the current zone into another zone with a little adjustment to the relationship. Things like more understanding, clearer expectations, and improved communications can quickly move clients from one zone to another. The key to moving clients between zones is to identify what it will take to move them toward a tighter, deeper, better relationship, and closer to joy. Identifying what may work allows you to create an action plan—and then actually implement it.

## ADEQUATE CLIENTS: TRANSACTION-DRIVEN + JOY = BLIP ZONE

**Adequate Clients** live inside the Blip Zone and are generally transaction-driven. Even though they are not necessarily the customers who want to know much about you, you probably like working with them because they are cool, easy to get work done with, and they can be repeat customers. Adequate clients don't generally cause issues or concerns, and they rarely take up any time outside of the actual transaction.

These clients are placed in the "Blip Zone" because they often result in a positive "Blip" (upturn) on revenue.

Melissa Noto, founder of Melissa Noto Design Studio in Illinois, provides graphic design services to her clients. "I have a lot of Park District clients who hire me for the year to design their activity program guides. I also have a lot of clients who hire me for individual projects here and there. It might be a logo, a brochure, or some website graphics, like one-off projects. I'll see them once, and they might come back later in the year or two years later for changes. I like it because it keeps me busy, and it's no big deal to just make a few changes. I already have the files, and it's nice to see them again."

In Noto's case, the clients are perfect "fill in the hole" clients. They provide revenue a few times per year because they trust her enough to continue to come back. Furthermore, they aren't demanding, and the work they need done is completed rather quickly.

Keep in mind that a client may be in the Blip Zone, but not in the Adequate section. When this happens, it's because the client brings you plenty of joy and causes you limited to no pain. When clients don't bring as much joy as expected or as much as you think they could, then they slip into the Adequate Zone.

## ARE ADEQUATE CLIENTS LIKELY TO MOVE?

Over time, you might be able to move these clients to the Great Client Zone, if you are able to move them from transaction-driven to relationship-driven. The key to moving them is to have conversations unrelated to any specific transaction. Talk about something related to who they are as a person. Try to learn more about them, what they do in their off time, and what is important to them. Specifically ask *them*, "What brings you joy?" and "What makes you happy?"

## IDENTIFIERS/RED FLAGS

You can look for a number of things that might place a client into either the Adequate Zone or the Blip Zone. They are:
- Limited to zero small talk
- No interest in you or others on your team

- Time is precious, no time for chit chat
- Rarely returns calls or check ins unless it's to place an order
- Makes you laugh or smile when you interact with them
- Never discusses payment options or pricing for your services
- Rarely, if ever, asks for discounts and most often pays what you ask

## CHALLENGING CLIENTS: TRANSACTION-DRIVEN + PAIN = NO-GO ZONE

**Challenging Clients** are transaction-driven people who tend to be frustrating to work with because they waste your time, are slow to pay, may be unethical, show disrespect, undervalue your work, don't follow processes, are less likely to refer, and want more work for less money. We place them in the "No-Go Zone" because they take too much time, make things difficult, and rarely result in a profit.

Jack Potter owns Potter Marketing & Branding in Florida. Being in business since 1972, he has had many clients and has the stories to prove it:

> We had a client we worked with very well on the first project, but it was rough because there was so much back and forth and rush deadlines. Rush deadlines can always be avoided if the planning is right. We pulled it off and succeeded. The second project came along. Again, they were late with everything. Toward the end, I started to "smell a sardine," if you will. I checked into them a bit further and found out the internal guy was their "creative director" and also their software developer. He was angry that I was doing the creative work he wanted to do. I was hired to correct all the problems. It turns out that during the second project, he brought in his own vendor and wouldn't give me any data. There was a price war, and at the end, I told my client that he should just go with the internal guy since they were already paying him.
>
> Some clients just don't work out.

## ARE CHALLENGING CLIENTS LIKELY TO MOVE?

Generally speaking, Challenging Clients aren't likely to move to other zones. In fact, we should be firing them like Potter did. However, like every rule, there are exceptions. If the Challenging Client is closer to the middle of the matrix, then you have a chance to move them to another zone. My recommendation is that you meet, in person if possible, to discuss the overall relationship. Open communication will tell you a lot about the person, where their mind is, and where their expectations lie. You really have one goal at this meeting: to determine if the relationship will continue or not. You need to be prepared to let the client go. That alone will ensure that you're ready to move on, and it will be up to them to convince you otherwise. Before you leave the meeting, clearly identify what each party needs to do moving forward to ensure you both enjoy working together. This business relationship should not be one-sided. If this meeting has a positive outcome, you have a chance of moving this client closer to the center of the matrix.

## IDENTIFIERS/RED FLAGS

You can look for a number of things that might place a client into either the Challenging Zone or the No-Go Zone:

- Clients have no idea about workload or how your services work.
- Obstinate, do not follow processes.
- After a couple of meetings, red flags confirm they are not the right fit.
- Clear feelings it is not the right fit, even when payment is presented.
- Start to feel as though you should walk away.
- At some point, you realize it's just not worth it.
- The client didn't want to attend meetings and handed them off to a colleague.
- No trust or unable to build and establish trust.
- Unrealistic expectations.
- Unethical.
- Disrespectful.
- Repetitive conflicts, defensive, combative, argumentative.
- Life-draining (demotivating, energy draining).
- Visible desperation coming from the client.
- Client plays games and/or plays the victim.
- Constrains the outcome or progress.
- Strategic interests misaligned.

- Your inability to smile when this client calls on the phone.

## RISKY CLIENTS: RELATIONSHIP-DRIVEN + SOME PAIN = HASSLE ZONE

**Risky Clients** tend to be relationship-driven and love relationships. They enjoy building the relationship, which is great, but that also can take a ton of time. While the relationship might be what we are looking for, it doesn't mix well when these clients cause you pain. That can show up in the form of their inability to pay or pay on time. This mixture causes pain, and often, a loss of profits. We place them in the "Hassle Zone" because they are quite the hassle.

"In general, clients who have both hands out to receive and never give anything back are not a good fit for me," explains Berta Medina, founder of Dreamers Succeed in Florida. "That becomes very clear as you get to know the people. I can coach them, and get them to do certain things, but at a certain point it's evident we are not aligned. If we can't be on the same page, I always refer them out. I'm always very loving. I'm always very generous with my grace and the transition. But if we are not aligned, it just becomes about money, and I don't operate that way."

In Medina's case, it becomes painful when the alignment is off. As she indicated, it's not always about money. The Hassle Zone is full of well-intentioned people who love to build relationships but often take more than they give. When I say take, I mean your time.

The clients who become a hassle often do so because they aren't following our processes/procedures. They begrudgingly go along as we drag them through the process. The more we pull on them, the more frustrated we get. Because these folks know how to build great relationships and have great conversations, we put them into the Risky Zone. These conversations keep business owners engaged in the overall relationship. The more problematic these clients are, the less likely we are to engage with them. As they start to move left on the pain scale in the matrix, they also start to drop down the grid toward transactional because we are less likely to continue building the relationship with them.

## ARE RISKY CLIENTS LIKELY TO MOVE?

**Risky clients** can be moved to other zones. The key here is to get them to bring us more *joy* and less pain. The more they slide right on the scale, the more likely they are to be Great Clients and even move into the Ideal Client Zone. To move these clients up the *joy* scale, start finding ways to get them to open up more. Get them to understand you are a business owner, you love the relationship you have with them, you really enjoy the conversations you have, and you appreciate all the things you learn from them. Then tell them that from time to time, working with them causes you some discomfort. Let them know specifically why that is. Perhaps it's slow payment or exceptionally long phone calls. Or it could be a long-winded email you get from them each week about all the things that are your fault. (Yes, that actually happens.) Once you have this conversation, you'll start to see the client shift a bit on the matrix, hopefully, for the better and toward more *joy*.

However, sometimes this conversation results in the client pulling back from the relationship, continuing to do the things they did before, and that change alone will drop them down to Challenging, and ultimately, off your client list.

Congratulations...you are now pruning your client tree!

## IDENTIFIERS/RED FLAGS

Clients can be moved into either the Risky Zone or the Hassle Zone based on several factors:
- Overstays their welcome on the phone or in person.
- Sends many unnecessary emails.
- Lacks attention to detail, resulting in difficult conversations and possibly unbillable work.
- Intriguing conversation on the phone—then you start checking your watch.
- Doesn't often recognize boundaries.
- Gets off track and constantly needs to be redirected back on track.

- Goes around the primary contact often to get your team to do things they want that are contradictory to your wishes and your process.
- Initiates workarounds and doesn't follow your process.
- Often fails to follow your process/procedures.

## GREAT CLIENTS: RELATIONSHIP-DRIVEN + JOY = IDEAL CLIENT ZONE

**Great Clients** are relationship-driven. They bring great satisfaction to your workplace because they don't cause you pain, they don't complain unnecessarily, and they pay their bills on time. They ask about your family and your social life. They are nice people, and you like to be around them. These clients are placed in the "Ideal Client Zone" because they bring you *joy*.

Earlier, we looked at stylist and salon owner Pauline Robertson's goals for good hair and great customer service. After years of being in business, she has developed loyal clients. "I was shut down for the first two weeks of quarantine for the COVID-19 pandemic." Knowing the drastic nature of losing so much income, she started calling her clients to see how she could help them. "I offered gift certificates and put together curbside hair color kit pickups, just to help me get money in the door." While picking up her kit, one of Robertson's customers said, "Pauline, I was supposed to have my hair done last week. You always do such good work. I'm going to pay you as if I had my hair done. Thank you for everything you do." Robertson exhaled. "Their loyalty and generosity covered all of my bills. It was incredible."

It gives me chills every time I hear this story. Robertson isn't the only person who has had clients show up for them when they needed them. COVID-19 produced many cases of this, as did the recession in 2008, and a myriad of other challenges that businesses have faced. The relationships we build with the people who bring us joy produce these stories. Not every client will pay Robertson for services they didn't receive; however, a much larger percentage of Ideal Client Zone ones will!

The Ideal Client Zone is a place of great value, not just for you, but also for your clients. When you have great relationships with amazing people, you'll often do more for them without them ever asking. Interestingly enough, that's exactly what they will do for you as well. Reciprocity is strong inside the Ideal Client Zone!

An interesting aspect of the Ideal Client is they are not always our most profitable clients because sometimes the best clients don't spend the most money. They are fun to work with and they are relationship-driven, but sometimes they just don't need many of our services.

Jared Grinkis, co-owner of Temp Secure Staffing in Massachusetts, said, "I have customers in every zone. The one thing that came to my mind is that our ideal client doesn't generate the most revenue. They are just good people we like working with."

I see this time and time again. It's important to be very clear: our Ideal Clients are *not* sorted by revenue or profit. They are determined by the relationships we have with them and the joy they bring to our work.

## ARE GREAT CLIENTS LIKELY TO MOVE?

Clients aren't likely to move out of the Great Zone too often. However, some in the great zone may do things you don't like or switch from relationship-driven to transaction-driven and slip out of the zone. If they start to slide left toward Risky on the matrix, it's because there is a bit less joy or a bit more pain. The key is getting to them sooner rather than later and having a brief conversation about what is going on. That will usually work to get things back on track.

Additionally, if you start to see them slip down the relationship scale toward transactional, start investing a bit more time into the conversations you have with them that are not focused on the services you offer. Instead, focus on them. This should bring things back into alignment and get them moving back up the matrix toward the great zone again. It's rare for clients to move out of the Ideal Client Zone, but it does happen. I've seen this occur most often when the relationship changes because a key person leaves the company and the relationship was actually with the person who left. It can also happen if the relationship goes south. When a client moves from the Ideal Client Zone, it's something you want to really take a look at. In my experience, I have found it's rare that the relationship can be saved. If you think it can be saved, take a hard look at it because sometimes the effort of bringing it back may not be worth the time. That's a choice you'll need to make on a case-by-case basis.

## IDENTIFIERS/RED FLAGS

You can look for a number of things that might place a client in either the Great Zone or the Ideal Client Zone:

- Collaborative, willing to do a deeper dive.
- Exchange/Share ideas.
- Credit is not an issue.
- They easily pivot and course correct.
- They respect, appreciate, and value your expertise, processes, and recommendations.
- Clear feelings—verbal, nonverbal, and internal—that the relationship is a good fit.
- The *first* interaction makes it evident they will be open to suggestions and they see that you, the service provider, can help them.
- They are excited to work on the next project or phase and attend meetings, take calls, and participate in conferences.
- Trust is present and clear.
- They are logical and rational.
- They are open, honest, and generally speak directly.
- They have ethical standards and are transparent.
- They believe in a mutually beneficial relationship.
- They are life-giving (energizing).
- Your values align.
- You have mutual buy-in.
- They allow for your autonomy.
- They understand the value in the products and services you offer.
- They offer constructive and helpful feedback and share their knowledge.
- They respect your role as their advisor and service provider.

Now that you've seen how we can use the Ideal Client matrix to understand where clients fall, as well as the identifiers and red flags, you can really start to paint the picture of what your business is like now and what you want it to be like. Use the matrix for clarity and as a guide to improving your overall client portfolio.

Using the matrix, plot your current clients. Write the names of ten clients in the numbered blanks. Then plot the corresponding number into the matrix where they fall. Continue this process until you have enough clients in the matrix to form an understanding of where your clients fall.

Do you see a pattern? What work needs to be done?

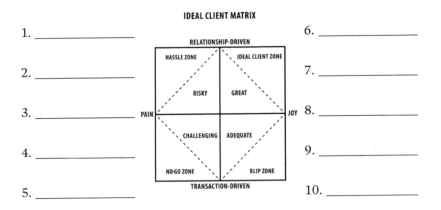

1. _____

2. _____

3. _____

4. _____

5. _____

6. _____

7. _____

8. _____

9. _____

10. _____

# CHAPTER 16

# EXPECTED RESULTS

Whether now or later, when you plot your clients on the Ideal Client Matrix, 60 to 70 percent most likely will fall near the center. Wherever they fall, try to identify if it's possible to move them closer to the Ideal Client Zone. Those who stay in the No-Go Zone or the Risky Zone need to be assessed to see if they can become better clients or if you are better off releasing them to someone else. "Releasing them" is a professional phrase for firing them and "referring them out" to a competitor. No matter the situation, you always want to maintain your professionalism. It's a small world, and you never want to burn a bridge.

Greg Mandile, owner of Mandile Web Design in Waltham, Massachusetts, said that roughly seven years ago he had a client who left under not-so-great terms. "The company was struggling, and I was helping them, but when it came time to pay, they couldn't. I offered them some payment options. They paid the first payment, then became unresponsive. Eventually, the company closed." Mandile went on to say, "Just recently, I received an email from this past client expressing remorse for not paying and letting me know there would be a referral coming from them. Sure enough, they sent over an email introduction for a referral in the next twenty-four hours. Since then, they have referred me two more times. I'm so glad I didn't burn that bridge."

Ultimately, the world is smaller than we think. We often realize through conversations that the person we are talking to might know people we already know. When that happens, our response is "Small

World." We also know that people talk, so don't react emotionally when clients frustrate you. Maintain your professionalism, and find a way to place them with someone else. They may eventually realize what they have done wrong.

Nicole Porter from Monomoy Social Media detailed her experience with a client. Let's just call this client..."Karen." Karen was quite challenging, and not Nicole's ideal client. In 2020, Nicole released Karen as a client. But that didn't keep Karen from continuing to reach out with requests and general emails. Within six months, Karen sent Nicole an email detailing her experience following the release. She went on to say she had been fired by the next two companies she had hired to manage her social media. While Karen did mention that Nicole's customer service was unprecedented and stood head and shoulders above the others, Karen never acknowledged how difficult of a client she was for Nicole, or these other companies.

Just because your client may find that your services are best for them does not mean they are the best client for you!

Your results, in your business, are based on your strength in addressing difficult clients and moving them to a positive location on the matrix or moving them off the matrix entirely.

The goal here is to have awesome clients who produce fruitful business where you gain more money, more time, and more freedom. And that is exactly why we are in business.

After six years in business, John Ela, a CEO coach from New Hampshire, created a formula for choosing his clients. When coaching CEOs, his goal is to help them lead better, build better organizations, and help their teams achieve the most important goals. See if you can pinpoint which zones his three types of clients fall into. Ela stated:

> The advantage to having [my] own business is I can decide whom I want to work with. Working with a lot of CEOs, I've identified that they really fall into three buckets. A lot of them are bullies, and I won't work with the bully because the best I can do is help them understand they are a bully. They are the problem, in which case, I'll be fired. They won't change anything, and nothing gets accomplished. Working with them is a waste of time.
>
> In the second bucket are those who think they are the smartest in the room. I can figure them out because they tell me all about

their certifications and about everything they've read. My challenge with them is they already have all the answers, so they don't need a coach to help them change. It's funny, because as I get them to talk about their challenges, it turns out their challenges are the very things they just preached to me about as though they are the expert. Plus, they also enjoy telling their peers they have a high-powered CEO coach.

Here, Ela chuckled, and that made me chuckle. I've seen those folks for sure!

The third bucket is my favorite. This group of CEOs is truly trying to find a better way. Being a CEO is a difficult job because they are always learning. It's a job unlike any other. All the hard problems bubble up to the top, so you're facing issues every day that you have never had before. You can either hunker down and say, "Well, I know all the answers," or you can try to find better answers. And those are the kinds of people I look for because I can have the most impact on them, and they are the most fun to work with.

Ultimately, there are two ways to get results from the Matrix.

1.  Thin the herd. Remove unwanted and difficult clients.
2.  Onboard more clients who are closer to your ideal client.

# CHAPTER 17

# NEXT STEPS

## Use the Ideal Client Matrix to Identify Future Ideal Clients

Looking at your matrix with your clients plotted on the graph, what do you see?

- Do you see any clusters?
- What do they tell you? Are there more risky clients or are there more adequate clients? Or do you have all great clients? Or are they all in the No-Go Zone? Hopefully, not the latter.
- What do the clusters tell you about your strengths, weaknesses, and value?
  - If the majority of your clients fall within the Ideal Client Zone, you are strong at recognizing which clients you want to have on your roster.
  - If more of them are in the Blip or Hassle Zone, what does that tell you about your willingness to work with difficult clients? As you think about the concentration in these areas, is the matrix speaking to you? Does it say anything about ending some contracts and opening new contracts that fit the Ideal Client Zone more?
  - How many are in the No-Go Zone?

If most of your clients are in the Blip, Hassle, or No-Go Zones, it's not the end of the world. Since you are a business owner in progress, you have the power to make changes. You know more now about your clients than you ever did. You will do better. Awareness often highlights some need for improvement, and then changes are often implemented. You are now able to see where your clients land, and you are able to move them from one quadrant to the next if you want to do the work. Remember, sometimes, it's not worth moving them, and you refer them to others.

As I work with my clients, I often use a magnet analogy when it comes to moving their clients toward the Ideal Client Zone. Imagine a horseshoe-shaped magnet. Position the magnet in the upper right of the matrix so it's just outside the matrix, but the ends touch the outside edges of the top and right side at the same time. Okay, great, got that image in your head? With your clients plotted on the matrix, imagine the magnet gently pulling the clients toward it from all the different zones. The farther away the clients are, the weaker the magnet will be. Some of those clients might be out of range of pull for the magnet and won't move at all. Some may move slightly while others may move more quickly. The farther away they are, the slower they will move toward the magnet.

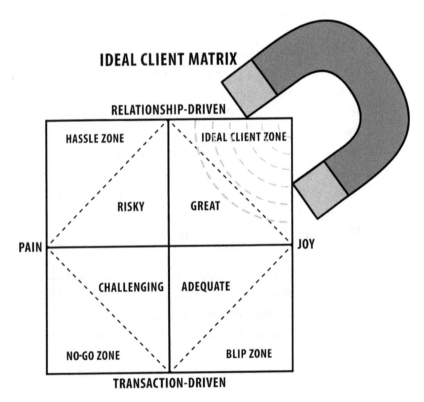

It's always a great idea to be thinking about what our next steps are for our business and specifically for the types of clients we want. Changes in the density of our clients will change over time, just by natural progression; however, it's always best if we can control the changes in client density and location in the Ideal Client Matrix to ensure we are getting the best fit clients. One of the best ways to do that is when we are acquiring new clients in our business.

# CHAPTER 18

# NEW CLIENTS

The Ideal Client Matrix is one tool you can use in client selection as you bring new clients into your business. You have confirmed which types of clients are challenging for you. You also know by the clients you have which ones bring you joy. Now, it's your decision how to proceed.

**Tips for Choosing Ideal Clients**
- Be extremely picky.
- The first interaction must prove they are open to suggestions and open to your help/expertise.
- Take five minutes after each meeting to replay the meeting and evaluate what was said and not said; identify any issues or matters left unsaid—those are the loudest screams we don't hear.
- Ask questions, many questions.
- Evaluate the source of the referral or how they found you—trusted friend, association, google search?
- Can you trust them?

Remember, to build a business where clients bring you *joy*, you'll need to make some hard decisions. The matrix and the lists provided throughout this phase are two resources for helping you find your ideal clients. The third and most interesting resource is coming up in the next phase: Strengthen. You will then have exactly what you need to find your ideal clients during your interview process, discovery, or sales calls. You will know immediately if the prospective client you are meeting with will become a client who causes you pain or brings you joy. Once you surround yourself with clients who bring you joy, you will achieve your desired goal of:

**MORE MONEY, MORE TIME, AND MORE FREEDOM!**

**ARE YOU READY TO STRENGTHEN YOUR BUSINESS?**

**LET'S GO!**

# PHASE IV

# CHAPTER 19

# IT'S GAME DAY!

*"No one, and I mean no one, comes into our house and pushes us around."* That's right, Coach Dan Devine. I still get a little teary eyed when I watch *Rudy*. Who doesn't? It's one of the greatest football movies ever. It takes me back to my days as a youth football coach. As a business coach, I've seen all the issues we've discussed. Many business owners just need a different perspective on some things, a little push of confidence, and some coaching to course correct.

Let me remind you...this is your business.

We all struggle through the same issues, whether it's messaging, processes, confidence, clients, or our own decision making. At some point during our tenure in business, it all comes together.

Whether it's right now or three years from now, I want you to take your power stance and say, "Enough is enough! *No one, and I mean no one, comes into my house and pushes me around."*

Yeah!

Your business is your house, and as Dan Devine said, no one comes in and pushes you around. The way to realize the success you envisioned when you opened your doors is right there in front of you, in the form of your clients, partners, and the people you surround yourself with. The people you work with and the clients who hire you are your family. Sure, you have some areas to tweak. You'll get that done. Maybe you need a confidence booster, and hopefully, this book will help you with that. *The High-Five Effect* model is designed to give you a new perspective and a new approach to building your house with a family that brings you *joy*!

In Phase 3: Identify, we explored the reasons you take on certain clients, the types of clients you may currently have on your roster, and how surrounding yourself with ideal clients will bring you *joy*. Now that you have the model to identify your ideal client "avatar," there are two more phases to cover: Strengthen and Engage.

Let's get started.

When I was coaching youth football, at the start of every football season, we had six weeks of training to prep for weekend games. The young, excited, and terrified players would act all cool walking away from their parents with their helmets in their hands toward the huddle.

On the first day, they looked at me with big doe-like eyes, terrified for their lives, worried they were going to get hurt. We started slow. First, we assessed their athleticism. Second, we recognized what they did well. Running, throwing, catching, passing, and blocking were the main skills we evaluated. Then, we praised them to boost their confidence, which helped them start to value themselves as players and value their contribution to the team.

We next identified their jersey numbers (always a big deal) and positions (even a bigger deal). Once we finished the roster, our next job was to strengthen their knowledge of the game, their relationships with their team members, and their skills. Picture sixteen nine-year-old boys of all heights, shapes, and athletic abilities out there doing exercises they never saw before, losing their step, missing the ball, running into each other, and feeling like losers for the day. Everything we learn playing sports, being on a team, and being in a competitive environment translates to what we need to do as business owners.

Our next play in this book is Strengthen. We need to strengthen your decision-making skills when it comes to choosing to work with clients who bring you *joy*. How hard can it be? It's actually not hard once you know the secret.

Through my coaching and networking, I've met so many business owners who struggle with the same issues. I've been there, and it drives me crazy to hear the same issues happening over and over again. I've been doing this long enough that I've learned how to identify the No-Go Zone clients during the prospecting process. However, it took me a long time, and I'm not alone. You are not alone. Strengthening your client identification process will be one of the best things you do as a business owner. As American journalist Hunter S. Thompson said, "Anything worth doing, is worth doing right."

I don't want people to be frustrated in business, nor be challenged and have problems with client acquisition because when that happens, business is no longer fun. And life becomes difficult.

## STRENGTHEN YOUR DECISION MAKING

*"People only change when the pain of not changing is so great there is no other choice."*

*— Larry Winget*

An important tip to remember as you transform old habits into new habits is: be flexible with yourself. You will not score a touchdown every time, so give yourself grace when dropping the ball. Just like those nine-year-old boys, the more practice, the more touchdowns. The more touchdowns, the more wins.

Change is never easy, especially when it comes to taking on clients so we can have a thriving business. As we discovered in the Client Acquisition Hierarchy of Needs and in the Identify Phase, we say "yes" to every client when we first start out. We learn lessons the hard way while realizing some clients just don't fit for myriad reasons. We get knocked down, brush off our knees, and get up again. It hurts. The cuts will heal. Over time, we start to recognize some of the familiar personality traits, behavior patterns, and signs we've learned don't fit into our ideal client profile. For some of us, it takes longer. We usually notice when it shows up on the profit and loss ledger, and then we see the fumbles, interceptions, and failed plays, which force us to make better decisions.

As Larry Winget said, change is going to come when you feel there is no other choice. Until then, we keep signing up less than ideal clients.

## MONDAY MORNING QUARTERBACK

Denise Pierce, founder of DP Performance Consulting in Massachusetts, bypassed her process for one client. "A colleague referred a new client to me from a networking group. She's an ethical person; she knew him, so I consider him a 'qualified lead.' He wouldn't pay the remainder of his bill, and I had to chase him for six months. Finally, I won the case in small claims court, but it reinforced for me to always follow my own process."

With some people, no matter the process you follow, it just isn't meant to work out. Jodi Crowley followed her processes with some new realty clients at Lamacchia Realty in Massachusetts. She described the situation as follows:

> I realized they were pretty picky, which describes most people looking for a house. When I work with people, I try to find people with similar values and similar approaches to life. I'm straightforward. I negotiate hard and try to get the best deals for my clients. Everything was going along, and when we got into the deal, it was like they flipped a switch and became extremely different people. I didn't see it coming. It was a difficult situation for the seller, and this couple was really pushing the envelope and taking advantage of the situation. I really didn't want to be working with them, and yet I had a fiscal responsibility to them. I did my due diligence; I did my job. But I will not stay in touch with them. I will not be working with them again, and I'm not interested in working with their friends or family.

It's definitely not easy to let clients go, and it takes even more guts to say no to money from a prospective client. I can relate to these stories from my experiences early on with my agency. In that first year, I was clearly in survival mode. I learned later that part of the reason my agency wasn't bringing in enough money for me to get the paychecks I wanted was because I attracted the wrong fish. These clients couldn't afford to hire bigger companies, so they came to me.

It got worse before it got better. I offered unlimited updates for website maintenance. Most people had a lot of changes early on, but then it would fizzle out to occasional updates, which was the original plan. However, one client called every day or two with pages and pages of changes. This went on for months. He was definitely in the Hassle Zone. Finally, I had to let him go and referred him out to some-one else. I had to stay true to the agreement I had with him; however, he was taking up far more of our time than any one person should. It was just too much. I figured I needed to connect him with someone who would take good care of him. I just didn't have the capacity to do it anymore, and with all my attention on him, I was losing money and risked potentially losing many other clients.

I was so desperate for cash, clients, and revenue that I ended up not charging enough for the products and services we offered. At that time, I didn't understand value, pricing, or competition. The lesson I learned was to always examine the market, do the SWOT (Strengths, Weaknesses, Opportunities, and Threats) analysis, and make sure your pricing includes your hard costs (rent, salary, etc.), your over-head (lights, admin, etc.), and your own paycheck before you offer the "blue light special" to get people in the door. That way, you know the minimum you need to charge for the services you offer.

It takes a while before we are comfortable turning clients away. It can even take a few years for us to emerge from the Security Stage. Eric Slivoskey owns a personal development company in North Dako-ta. He discusses how to move past the scarcity mindset of this stage:

> When we don't know where the next client is coming from, we operate in a scarcity mindset that doesn't serve us well. Within a couple of years of starting my business, I realized my services aren't for everyone. That doesn't mean it's a reflection that my business is faulty or problematic. It means I've created more self-awareness in me and my own expectations. I know my customer avatar. I know who I can help and the problems I can solve. It helped me when I defined my mission and focused on the out-comes, results, and quality control.

## THE PASS IS GOOD...TOUCHDOWN!

Fortunately, not all relationships are challenging, and our great clients help us learn who we want to have in our playbook. Rob Rains, founder of Certissima Technologies in Massachusetts, offers managed IT services and security services. He describes what great clients are for him:

> My favorite client is a financial services firm because they are involved. They listen to our advice. They ask questions because they like to know what's going on. And they even follow our advice and say, hey, we're really grateful. Because they understood what we were doing, they were able to connect the dots realizing that there would have been major problems without our services. The bonus is that they refer us to clients, which is cool.
>
> For us, our best IT and security clients are those who want to be involved and know what's happening, and they trust us enough to hand over the keys to the kingdom. They let us do our job. The likeness goes both ways. Reporting updates on progress has been key to remind them of the value we bring. We've also learned they really appreciate a report that updates them on the work, the results, and how it relates to the fees.

Keith Reardon, founder of Commonwealth Consulting Group in Massachusetts, moves money for his clients. His best client is a brewery. "They are just awesome people who value the work we do and the service we provide." The client repeatedly refers his company, too. "Ultimately," Reardon says, "I think it's relationships, you know, and having that human connection with somebody versus just the business connection. Obviously, we are the business connection, but when it's good people, you enjoy working with them, they respect you, they know who you are, and what you do, so it doesn't feel like business; it feels like family."

Denise Pierce reminds me that in any game, the field has to be playable. "Till your garden." In football, someone is responsible for the maintenance of the playing field. "A friend of my dad's shared his philosophy with me: Listen, your business is like a garden. You're either going to have weeds in it, or you're going to grow flowers and plants that will prosper. And if you don't pull out the weeds, they'll overtake your garden." Smart advice for any business owner. Pierce continued:

> I always look at every prospect as a potential client and ask (myself, of course), are you a flower? Are you going to be a weed? Are you going to drain me dry and take me on a wild goose chase? Or are you going to overextend my services and not want to pay for

certain things? Or will we have a mutually beneficial relationship? If the answer is "Flower. We're both going to grow, and it'll be a win-win." Then, that's the client who brings me *joy*!

A few years ago, I bought a laptop without talking to more than one person. I bought it from Mike Kimball at Computer Central. It was a $1,400 purchase. Certainly, there are many laptops, configurations, and prices. However, I never shopped around because I've known him for a long time. There's a relationship there; I trust him; he's a great guy and fun. Based on our relationship, I wanted to support his business. However, as we identify the types of clients we have, it makes me wonder what type of client am I to vendors or the people I interact with daily? Most likely, for Mike, I was in his Blip Zone because I don't buy monthly plans or services from him. In fact, he primarily fixes computers and sells new ones. His exchanges are often more transactional than relational. However, building a relationship with Mike over the years, I know his hobbies, and I know more about his family. While that isn't a relationship with a lot of interaction, it's definitely not at the bottom of the transaction scale.

## FLAG ON THE PLAY: UNNECESSARY ROUGHNESS

There's stuff we put up with in the early days because we need revenue. We need a baseline. We need security. We need to survive. Right? We may not like it, but we tell ourselves, "Okay, I know difficult clients are worth the extra money." But then we graduate to say, "I respect myself way more than that. I respect what I do. I have respect from my community and respect from my industry. I'm not interested in dealing with your unnecessary roughness. I don't care if you pay me three times my fees. I'm just not interested."

Pravin Shekar, founder of Krux108 in India, is well-known for his unconventional marketing strategies. He describes a bad client situation:

> The worst client was the one who had a lot of dreams and aspirations, but absolutely no idea about marketing or the amount of work needed to get his business running. He was absolutely obstinate. In terms of not listening to the suggestions, he wanted to get everything done immediately. The work he was asking to

do could never get done in the short time frames he was giving me. He refused to listen to anything I advised, and he just wanted someone to get it done.

This kind of client behavior I term "unnecessary roughness."

We start noticing we made a bad call when the red flags are flying (almost like penalty flags in a football game), and we find that our relationship with the client is clearly fumbling. If we are not in the heat of it, we can step away and recognize it as unnecessary roughness. And once we are willing and able to say, "I've had enough," we reach the fifty-yard line. We have found respect for ourselves. That's what takes us halfway there. We are more confident that we are ready to select great clients instead of taking on everyone with a need and a check. The latter would definitely fall into the No-Go Zone. We value ourselves. And now, we are on our way to scoring better clients more often and able to say to others, "Take a hike."

## PASS OR PLAY

By now, you have experience with many types of clients. You've had some good plays and some you wish you would have passed on—if only you had known...that one thing was going to happen...or if you would have just read the signs. Where were those signs? Why didn't someone warn you? Why couldn't you figure it out yourself?

Pravin Shekar, founder of Krux108, said, "I started working with my toughest client ever. After a couple of 'dating sessions,' I politely said, 'I'm not the right person to work with you.'"

Darik Eaton, owner of Seattle Oasis Vacation Rentals, states: "My clients have taught me that I am responsible for getting them in the right mindset about their property, and now it's what I do best." Although Eaton never played organized football, he knows how to be a team player. Eaton's company is a vacation rental management firm. His job is to turn homes into vacation rentals. It can be incredibly challenging, as he describes:

> When clients come to me, it's my job to help them get comfortable. They start out really possessive and concerned about their home. They say, "This is my home; I don't want anything bad to happen to it." Then, I have to get really uber-clear that when

they hand over the property, it becomes an investment property. I walk them through the detachment phase. They start to understand that stuff is going to go wrong, and we'll have to fix it with touch up paint, replace glass, and do maintenance of all sorts. I encourage them, "This is no longer your home, but under our watch, we are going to print you money! And that's the job of an investment property."

That's an ideal scenario for Eaton's property owners. On the other side of the vacation rental business, sometimes it's not ideal.

If the renters are asking about hypoallergenic pillow covers, I know they are not going to be an easy rental client. Or if they call to talk to me and they ask all the questions when all the answers are on the website, it's clear that they didn't read the property listing, so I just turn these people away. Chances are nothing is going to be good enough for them, and they are not going to read the contract and pay attention to details.

It's interesting how many lessons we learn from being in business for just a few years. Interviewing all these business owners was really enlightening, and I expected a variety of answers. Some surprised me, especially the common responses.

"I would say when people start asking for discounts, that's the first red flag," says Rita Beckly, owner of Timberwolf Vacation Rentals in Missouri. She runs into the same problems as Eaton. "I mean, asking for a discount alone isn't bad, but when they start asking questions that I've already clearly defined in the listing, that's a deal breaker. It means they haven't read the details and aren't going to take care of the property."

Rule bending and rule breaking (especially overcrowding) are a common issue in the vacation rental space, as both Eaton and Beckly explained. These are all red flags, and they have learned over time how to recognize them and not do business with red-flag people.

The key to strengthening your ability to make better decisions lies in your ability to look back on the decisions you've already made and identify the lessons. As you continue to grow in business, you'll run into more and more situations that are "firsts" for you. How you handle those firsts determines how quickly you will strengthen your skillset. Skills are perfected over time with repetition. You can shorten the time frame by spending more time on the skill and making it better.

My advice is to reflect on decisions you've made each day, and ask yourself, "What, if anything, could I have done differently?" That will fast-track you to developing more strength for when you need it in your business.

# CHAPTER 20

# YOUR INTERNAL BUSINESS COACH

If people aren't transparent from the beginning, it always foreshadows issues ahead. I completely understand Rita Beckly's concern. How do we recognize when clients aren't being truthful? How do we know they won't match our customer avatar? How do we know that while they seem cool, they will definitely end up in the No-Go Zone? "I always follow my gut," Beckly states matter-of-factly.

Follow your gut? Does that work? Do you ever feel a tug at your gut when evaluating whether the prospect in front of you, on the phone, or on the screen is your ideal client? Some people call it a gut feeling, some call it instinct, and some call it intuition. I call it a "common phenomenon." In fact, the majority of business owners I interviewed use it as a tool for their business, and I found that it directly correlates to the ability to grow your business, have the right clients, and find joy!

"We have more neurotransmitters in our body than in our brain that are communicating to us constantly," explains Angela Buttimer, a licensed psychotherapist from Atlanta. She is the founder of Atlanta Center for Mindfulness and Well-Being. "However, today, we don't recognize it because we are overextended and overstimulated, and we are not tuning into what our body is telling us."

"I always go with my gut," Denice Pierce said. When I asked, "You always go with your gut?" she confirmed, "Oh, yeah. I always go with my gut. My gut never steered me wrong. Never. So, I believe I have very good intuition as to reading people and knowing if it's going to be a good fit or not. I've walked away from people and said, 'No, I'm sorry, we are not a good fit.' I didn't instantly recognize my gut was talking to me. I built it up over time because it was something I had to recognize and acknowledge. It was always there. I just didn't listen to it."

Dr. Beth Plachetka, MA, MSW, LCSW, EdD., told me, "Our gut is always there. It's not that we learn *how* to listen to it; rather we ignore it. So, we need to learn *how to stop* turning it off." What? I almost fell off my chair when she explained the differences between gut feeling, instinct, and intuition (see below). It's such a powerful message. It's less about finding it, or listening to it, and it's all about our ability to stop turning it off. Who knew?

Plachetka further explains, "There are different connotations between gut feeling, instinct, and intuition. People use them interchangeably, but they are distinctly different." Plachetka then went a bit deeper to share the distinction:

- Instinct is the intent to stay alive.
- Intuition is when you sense something without having evidence.
- Gut feeling is a physical sensation, to me, that's saying "pay attention."

"I think I was trusting at first, and sometimes I was off," Beckly said, honestly and openly. "For me, it's a combination of experience and trusting my gut. I definitely trust my gut more now. It took a while."

According to Dr. Plachetka, it's good that Beckly trusts her gut more. "We know that the system is designed to keep us alive. So, when you walk into a dark alley or even brightly lit alleys and you get that feeling, 'I need to get out of here,' it's telling you there is a problem."

Plachetka recently had a situation at her therapy practice. "I knew in my gut, even though all logic told me something different, that I should not schedule an appointment with this particular person. My gut was screaming, 'no' while my brain was talking my gut out of it. So, when you ask, 'How do we develop it?' Actually, it's how do we stop ignoring it?"

As I listened to Plachetka, I reflected on the three inconspicuous phenomenon within our own internal systems. I recalled that during the time I spent running my agency, I never trusted my gut early on because I didn't think it was an "official business tool" for making business decisions. Then, as it showed up more and more in my day-to-day operations, I started following it, and realized I needed to trust it more. I figured, "I'm going to trust that my instinct is telling me that I don't want that client." But it wasn't my instinct, it was my gut emitting a physical sensation saying, "pay attention." If the client had a knife, now that would be instinct because I would be in fear for my life. Luckily, that never happened, and let's hope it never does.

If a client does come at me with a knife (although, I would prefer they throw me a football), Joyce Marter, LCPC, founder of Joyce Marter Enterprises, Inc. and of Urban Balance, Inc., assures me that my instincts will kick in. "We are biologically primed to respond to stressors such as flight, fight, freeze, or fawn mode." Fawn mode is a rather new concept that describes a codependency response for those who feel they are in danger and must please others to get out of it.

All of this made me wonder how our body and mind process red flags. As a psychotherapist working with adolescents, adults, and couples, Dr. Plachetka has red flags come up quite a bit. She states:

> Red flags actually send out electromagnetic kinds of sensations. This is called proprioception, and we also have an internal section that makes us pay attention to the inside of our body. At the same time, we're paying attention to the outside of our body, and that is all unconscious. That's the stuff that's keeping us alive, keeping our body alive while the spirit and soul is doing what it's supposed to be doing. Those red flags come when there's some kind of energetic piece that doesn't line up with you. There are all kinds of reasons someone may not jive with you. It could be that it's blatantly contrary to what we want. Sometimes we are not going to get along with everyone. But that really goes back to your gut. It's a sensation that feels like it could be a "red flag." That's a colloquialism, for there was a sign and the sign was in you.

So do the red flags, instincts, intuition, and gut feelings, all work together? According to Dr. Plachetka:

> Your instinct will recognize it because that's the desire to stay alive, and your intuition says you know something without evidence, which also gives you that sensation. Here's how it plays out. Say there is a person in a nice suit, looking good, smelling good. All that good stuff comes in, and right away I have that sensation. I have no evidence, none. But that sensation is intuition. I know I'm going to have to pay attention and follow my "gut." The words themselves are synonymous, but with the physical sensation, it's intuition—a thought without basis.

The important lesson is to be sure we pay attention to our body's signals. Often we just ignore it; we push it down and say it's wrong. If you say something's wrong long enough, it just gets louder. Stop explaining it away. In order to be in tune with our body, we need to make space for it, which means we need to take time each day to just be present and aware of what's happening around us and what our bodies are telling us about what is going on in our day and in our life.

Psychotherapist Joyce Marter agrees that listening to our body is vital so we don't miss important signals. She states:

> When we develop greater connection and awareness of the body through mindfulness practices like deep breathing, progressive muscle relaxation, and yoga, we increase our awareness. It's our thinking that gets us off track sometimes because we have this "mind chatter." A lot of it is based on our biases or what we want to see. Or our defense mechanisms can prevent us from picking up on things. So, if we check in with the wisdom of the body, there's a lot of information to access that can give you answers.

The conversations about following your gut were so interesting. It was fascinating that it took time for people to learn to trust their guts. I think, sometimes, small business owners feel since they didn't take a class in college called "Gut Feelings," they shouldn't use gut feelings as a business tool. In fact, what happens is we don't trust our gut early, and then, we start to trust it. As we have more and more experience, we build up that gut muscle, so to speak. We start to really trust it.

Sonja Stetzler, a communications and public speaking coach with Effective Connecting in North Carolina, said, "I learned to use gut instinct and built confidence from that. I don't come from a point of desperation and that's important because it makes my decision making clearer."

I picture this as using the weights in the gym to strengthen our gut.

# CHAPTER 21

# PLAYBOOK FOR PROSPECTIVE CLIENTS

Did you ever think your nervous system could work as hard as it does during initial discussions with clients? I certainly didn't. How do we really capitalize on what could be the secret of the century? Okay, maybe it isn't really, but it's probably close. Psychotherapist Joyce Marter advises:

> When we meet someone for the first time or second time to see if we are a good fit, we need to prepare ourselves to be present and aware in the present moment. It puts you in a higher sense of consciousness, so our ideas and feelings are waves of energy that we experience in the body. Become attuned to those feelings in your own body in the presence of someone else. If you feel anxious or you're suddenly sitting differently, making yourself feel small, sitting up, laughing, and reaching out are all signs about how well you will or will not work together.

*"Who wants to sit in the cauldron of indecision?"*

*— Matt Ward*

Remember Jodi Crowley from Lamacchia Realty? When she meets prospective clients, she schedules an *interview*, not a meeting. "I call it an interview before even taking buyers out to look at properties. And then

I follow up with them after because it gives me a chance to reflect and make sure we are a good fit."

I really like the idea of calling it an interview because I think people will take it a bit more seriously and understand it's a two-sided evaluation. To best prepare for the interview, Marter recommends turning off the mind chatter when we need to pay attention. "Being mindful is observing your self-talk, your physical processes. Cognitive behavioral therapy says that our thoughts proceed our emotions and behaviors. If we have catastrophic thinking, it's going to fuel anxiety and stress."

When it comes time to negotiate, Marter recommends further preparation.

> Do some reflective work on your self-esteem to see how you are feeling about this. Get a coach or therapist, if needed, to build on your strengths. It's so helpful to become your most confident self. Before you negotiate, know your minimum requirements, your boundaries of what you will do and will not do. Know the terms of your fee, availability, and schedule. Role play to practice your responses. For instance, "I'm sorry, I can't go below....

Knowing those factors *is* half the battle of a strong negotiation. You must always have your playbook ready.

As Pravin Shekar, founder of Krux108, enthusiastically shared his "process" with me, I could tell he truly relies on external cues beyond the discussion. "My gut definitely has something to do with it. But it's also the body language. How is the client moving? What are they saying? Am I lighting up on the inside about this project? You know, some meetings, you are charged up before you go in, and you're charged when you come out. But there are some you try to avoid. The minute you question the meeting, or you want to delegate it to someone else, it is a sure sign that something isn't right."

When I talked to Eric Slivoskey, we hit it off. During our chat, he said something I found very powerful. It stopped me in my tracks and I asked him to repeat it.

*"When your heart and your mind get into a tug of war. Let your gut settle it."*

— *Eric Slivoskey*

Like Shekar, Rob Rains, owner of Certissima Technologies in Massachusetts, uses more than his gut to determine whether or not he wants to work with a prospective client. "I'll be honest; I like to try to have my heart and mind going in the same direction. When that happens, I know it's moving in the right direction."

I would have to agree with Rains that the best way to pick a client is to have the heart and mind on the same side of fence. Curious, I asked Rains what he does when it's not on the same side of the fence. He replied:

> Like you said, "Let your gut decide." In my case, I call that a vibe. I've learned through the years that some of that vibe comes from experience, and some of it comes from reading nonverbal cues. Looking at body language, listening to the tone of their voice, watching their eye contact. But it's also experiential cues. For instance, when a prospect says, "If you give me a lower price now, I'll bring you more business later." In all my years, I've never, ever had that come to fruition. That's always a lie. And so, when someone says it, and this is my style, I'll gently call it out because I'm a very honest person. I know my style isn't for everybody. I expect other people to be transparent as well. So, I just call it out, and I say, "Hey, no offense. I've never seen that come to fruition. So, let's take that off the table. And let's look at what you can actually do." Then, we are able to talk about real numbers. I

always offer, "Instead of a discount now, if you send some business my way in the future, I'll give you a commission." It's fair, it's respectful, and it works.

Funny enough, I did the exact same thing in my agency. Both Rains and I saw the same behavior, promises of additional sales in exchange for discounts, and we both ended up handling it the same way.

Let's look at what he did. He asserted his confidence, self-respect, expertise, knowledge, terms, and he valued himself. He also unintentionally moved his prospect from the No-Go Zone to the Ideal Client Zone (temporarily, until he has the full picture).

Eric Slivoskey's quote above was well-received by every person I shared it with. Angela Buttimer was impressed by it and offered her opinion, "The heart can be too soft, and the mind doesn't want to throw anything away. Wisdom and clarity lie in the gut. The heart and mind become fused."

Like football, business has many rules, plays, losses, and wins. The key is to recognize the plays we learn as a business owner and those we learn from others. I know through writing this book and interviewing all these cool people that I've learned a great deal.

Pravin Shekar started to listen to his gut after three or four relationships that didn't go anywhere. He told me:

> Don't ask me about the scientific process of following your gut. I learned to hold a meeting with myself after each meeting and replay it in my head. I sit in silence just replaying the meeting to see if it is something I want to continue or not. I listen to the cues in my mind, body, and gut. At the end of five minutes, I know whether to onboard them as clients or walk away. The ability to walk away is necessary because I prefer to work with clients who are open to ideas, who are open to newer opportunities and experiments. In marketing, there are no guarantees, so I need my clients to be open to looking at failure as an option. This is marketing; not everything is going to work out fine.

In addition to Shekar's review process, Joyce Marter adds, "When you replay the meeting, see where your body is talking to you. Is it feeling anxious, nervous, down, exhausted? Are you feeling happy, fulfilled, or excited?"

Kimanne Foraker-Koons, an experiential therapist, mediator, and founder of Family Strategies Counseling and Mediation, operates her private practice in Illinois. The practice specializes in trauma. Foraker-Koons said, "When we are presented with options that are not good or ideal, we rationalize those thoughts ourselves even when we know the right decision. Other factors that feed into our decision-making could be past experiences in business, hurting someone's feelings, or having the fear of looking foolish."

I asked Shekar what advice he would have for new business owners who feel their gut speaking to them but also have a need for revenue. He said, "Take notes of every interaction, for what was said, and what was unsaid." Shekar feels the things not said are just as important as the things said, and that is why he recommends taking five minutes after each interaction to just be still and think about the interaction as a whole. That allows your gut to provide more feelings and your mind to be more in tune with your gut.

Shekar went on to say, "If I document our interactions for six months, then after that time frame, I will have some data to look back on. I'll also have some revenue from a number of clients, and at this point I can review the data I've collected from each engagement to substantiate my gut feeling. Furthermore, if I have other key stakeholders, then I have data to back up my gut and show to others."

Now that we know how instinct, intuition, and the gut fire off messages to us, we know to trust those messages. Your body tells you whether your prospective clients are No-Go or Ideal Clients. Stop the mind chatter, listen to your body, and make the call, like the All-Star quarterback you are! These are all methods to strengthen your gut feelings, your new secret business tool that will help you make stronger decisions for your business and bring you...

## MORE MONEY, MORE TIME, AND MORE FREEDOM!

The strengthen phase is the Super Bowl of brain dumps. Many of the people I interviewed have a process for determining the next step after a prospect call. It's clear to me the best practice is for each of us to identify the yes/no list of who we want to work with along with a list of the red flags that put someone in the No-Go Zone. Once you do these two steps, you'll be able to identify those prospective clients as ideal clients more quickly and easily. Then, our next play in the playbook is to identify all the methods of engaging our ideal clients.

## ARE YOU READY TO ENGAGE? LET'S GO!

# PHASE V

# CHAPTER 22

# ENGAGE YOUR CLIENTS

"Hey, I negotiate million-dollar deals for breakfast. I think I can handle"...*The High-Five Effect*! *Die Hard* is my all-time favorite movie. It's been around for more than thirty years and was the number eight most watched movie on December 1, 2020, according to CraveYourTV.com. Bruce Willis plays a New York City policeman named John McClane. On Christmas Eve, he joins his estranged wife for a holiday party hosted by her company. The event is interrupted by a group of pseudo-terrorists who take over the exclusive Nakatomi Plaza. McClane realizes there's no one to save the hostages—except him.

And that's you running your own business. You are the hero in your business. We don't run a business to blow it up intentionally, like John McClane did, but we sure do take extraordinary measures to keep our businesses running. We also look for methods to improve them, like you are doing here. Engage is how we work with the clients through communications, processes, and execution of what we want.

One of McClane's great lines in *Die Hard* was, "Welcome to the party, Hans!" Our goal here is not to let a customer into our Christmas party (our business) and let them steal our *bearer bonds* (our Joy).

Ask yourself, "What am I giving up by taking this opportunity?" John Ela offers these intriguing approaches as options to attain clarity. "Sometimes, your answer will flush it out and help you make a decision. You may still never get a clear answer, but you can get a greater sense of the dissonance between your heart and your head that's telling you something. Listen."

As you engage more with your clients, pay attention to what they say and how they act. More importantly, pay attention to your thoughts, feelings, and gut intuition.

You've got to get reps in! It's the consistency of engaging with your clients that really helps your business run at full speed!

Welcome to the party!

# CHAPTER 23

# CONTINUOUS IMPROVEMENT

One thing I see often with small business owners is this idea that if we learn something and take some action, that solves our problem. Too often, though, that is *not* the reality. The reality is, it's a philosophy of continuous improvement, over time, that establishes the standards within a company and result in an overall growth trajectory.

Ask yourself, "What systems and processes can we put in place now that will help us continue to engage our partners, prospects, and clients and serve them best while also serving our goal of achieving more joy in our business?"

In addition to gaining a one-percent change when I shitterate something, as I mentioned before, I'm always looking to automate something each week in my life. That also includes my personal life. I have found that over the years if I can streamline my personal life, it declutters my head for my business life. Therefore, I look at each week as an opportunity to improve or automate one system or process in my business or life. That is my process of continuous improvement.

*"If you want to produce great results in your business, you need to be consciously improving how well you do what you do."*

*— Bill Stainton*

# SO NOW WHAT?

We have now explored and examined all five phases of *The High-Five Effect*. We can compare the effort of implementing these five phases to the five steps of riding a bike for the first time.

**Step 1:** When we first purchase a bike, we sit on it, we test out the pedals, we check for the appropriate height, and we feel the handlebars. We are assessing the equipment, much like we assessed the important elements of our businesses. **Phase 1: Assess.**

**Step 2:** The most important aspect of riding a bike or anything worth doing is valuing ourselves. What we know, how we have prepared, and how confident we feel is important because it will help us have the courage to try something new, learn how to adjust, and keep trying. We slide our feet on the pedals, adjust our position on the seat, grab the handlebars, and push off to gain momentum. **Phase 2: Value.**

**Step 3:** As we start to gain momentum, we feel wobbly on the bike. We identify the source of the imbalance and crush the fear of falling, then adjust ourselves to eliminate the risk of falling. **Phase 3: Identify.**

**Step 4:** Our comfort level increases, we become more confident, we are now steady riders who have to shift gears and strengthen the push to climb up the next hill. As we stare through the middle of the handlebars, we see the top of the hill. **Phase 4: Strengthen.**

**Step 5:** As we crest the top of the hill and head down the other side, we realize all the bumps along the road have now smoothed out, our business is aligned. Just as we start down the hill, we feel the energy boost, the wind at our back. We get into an aerodynamic tuck. This is where we have less resistance and require less effort. We gain momentum, and now it's easier to make adjustments. With the wheels moving at a fast pace, we make minor adjustments that produce maximum results. We are ready to engage our clients full steam ahead on a much smoother street with fewer potholes, with people waving, smiling, achieving goals, and high-fiving everyone they meet. **Phase 5: Engage**.

Business is like riding a bike. When you fall off, you get up, get back on the bike, and try again. At times, we will need to pump the brakes to slow down a bit and correct our course, and that's okay, too. As long as you make forward progress, you are heading in the right direction.

*"I have learned there are three things in life. Do what you love, be with the people you love, and live in a place you love."*

— *Elaine Simpson*

Ultimately, you are the only one who can choose to build a business with clients who bring you *joy*.

**As I say on all my YouTube videos...**

**Are you ready?**

**LET'S GO!**

# Customer Profile Worksheet

Client Name: _____

Instructions: Quickly think about the client and what a day in the life of this client or customer looks like. Write down your thoughts.

## Questions

1. A day in the life of... What time do they get up?
2. A day in the life of... Where do they go?
3. A day in the life of... Where do they work or what do they do?
4. A day in the life of... What activities do they do?
5. A day in the life of... Who do they see?
6. Think about their lifestyle and why they have worked with you before. What's most important to them?
7. Think about why they worked with you and what was their problem that they needed to find a solution. What is their biggest challenge? What's bothering them today?
8. Think about what is on their dream list, what are the things they would do first when they meet that big goal. If money were no object, what's the first thing they would do/buy?
9. What social media do they scroll through?
10. What do they google?

11. What makes them happy?
12. What is the outcome they are looking for?
13. What is their age?
14. What, if any, social status do they have?
15. What is their education level?
16. What is their family dynamic, etc.?
17. Where are their eyeballs throughout the day?
18. What is their why?

Reprinted with Permission from Ronii Bartles

# INDEX

## A

accountability group, 48
Adequate Clients, 16, 91–92
Agin, Frank, *i*
Ahtof, Gina, *ii*
Alexander, Larry, *ix*
Assess phase
   about, 141
   in business owner's evolution of joy, 8, 11
   Client Acquisition Hierarchy of Needs, 23–30
   Discovery Stage, 28–29, 49–54
   Joy Stage, 28–29, 61–64
   Respect Stage, 28–29, 55–59
   Security Stage, 28–29, 41–48
   Survival Stage, 28–29, 31–39
Atlanta Center for Mindfulness and Well-Being, 123

## B

Bartles, Ronii, *i*, 36–37, 39
Beckly, Rita, 121, 123, 124
Blaney, Beth, *iii*
Blip Zone, in The Ideal Client Matrix, 91–92, 105
body language/signals
   paying attention to, 126
   of prospective clients, 130
Bounce-Back Effect, 69
boundaries, setting, 39
Brand, JuLee, *ix*
business community awards, 56–57
business journey, phases of, 8–12
business owners. *See also* specific people
   evolution of joy for, 7–12
   getting advice from, 33
   journey to joy, 19

## Y